The Customer Service Workbook

Other titles available in the Business Enterprise Guide series, published in association with *The Sunday Times* and the Institute of Directors, include:

The Business Enterprise Handbook: A complete guide to achieving profitable growth for all entrepreneurs and SMEs
Colin Barrow, Robert Brown and Liz Clarke

The Business Plan Workbook, Fourth Edition
Colin Barrow, Paul Barrow and Robert Brown

E-Business for the Small Business: Making a profit from the Internet
John G Fisher

Financial Management for the Small Business, Fifth Edition
Colin Barrow

Starting a Successful Business, Fourth Edition
Michael J Morris

Successful Marketing for the Small Business: A practical guide, Fifth Edition
Dave Patten

THE SUNDAY TIMES

BUSINESS ENTERPRISE GUIDE

The Customer Service Workbook

NEVILLE LAKE & KRISTIN HICKEY

RECOMMENDED BY

INSTITUTE OF DIRECTORS

KOGAN PAGE

First published in 2002

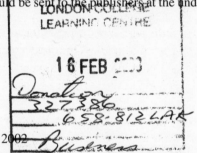

Kogan Page Limited
120 Pentonville Road
London N1 9JN
United Kingdom
www.kogan-page.co.uk

British Library Cataloguing in Publication Data

A CIP record for this book is available from the British Library.

ISBN 0 7494 3789 8

Typeset by JS Typesetting Ltd, Wellingborough, Northants
Printed and bound in Great Britain by Clays, St Ives plc

Contents

About the authors   vii

Preface   ix

Acknowledgements   xi

1. **Getting into your customers' heads, and winning their hearts**   1
    Why you need to understand your customers 2; What you need
    to understand about your customers 3; Decision-making
    processes 12; Desire for control 16

2. **Getting the facts through straightforward research**   20
    Observation 20; Experiencing 22; Talking 22; Internal
    research – qualitative 26; Internal research – quantitative 38;
    External research 40; Advanced research 41

3. **Making three big decisions, and building your service strategy**   42
    The three key ingredients for designing a service strategy 43;
    Implementing your service strategy 56; Using measures to stay
    on track 71

4. **Extraordinary performance from 'ordinary' people**   77
    Selection 78; Training 85; Customer-centred management 89

5. **Creating the culture that compels great service**   102
    The drivers of culture 103; Frontline empowerment 110

6. **Using the positive power of complaints** 119
Free research 120; The opportunity to improve broken
processes 123; The chance to recover – and create a story 125

7. **Making it all work** 129
Service processes 129; Service functionality and design 134;
Process improvement 151

8. **Location, location, location** 154
Context 155; Economics 155; Demography 156; Site
attributes 156; Geographic representation 159

9. **Measuring your performance** 165
Measuring customer satisfaction 165; Developing and
implementing service standards 184; How to use measures to
improve performance 190

10. **Customers who come back again and again and again** 196
What is loyalty? 197; How to measure loyalty 199; How to
develop loyalty strategies 204; What is the value of loyalty? 207

Appendix: Worksheets 210

References 217

Index 219

About the authors

Neville Lake is a Registered Psychologist who has spent the past 17 years as a business and strategic consultant. Neville has worked for three of the world's largest consulting firms, spending close to 10 years as a Director in the consulting division of Price Waterhouse. He established his own business – The Lake Group – in 1998.

Neville has developed a unique understanding of how businesses work through visits to over 50 world best-practice organisations, including British Airways, Coca-Cola, Citibank, Disneyland, Federal Express, Harrods, McDonald's, Ritz-Carlton, Rolls-Royce and Shell. He has consulted to over 80 businesses and has studied over 750 organisations. Neville is one of only three people in the world to have designed and written a major international benchmarking/best practice study on customer service.

Neville is the author of four other highly acclaimed management books. These include *The Third Principle: How to get 20% more out of your business*, which shows that virtually every organisation performs at no more than 80 per cent of its potential. In the book Neville provides unique diagnostics that describe the ways to identify trapped potential and he then reveals the techniques needed to remedy sub-optimisation.

He has also written *The Strategic Planning Workbook*, which is part of this *Sunday Times* series of Business Enterprise Guides. This practical and pragmatic workbook details Neville's unique approach to developing and implementing a straightforward strategic plan. This book made publishing history by including a 40-minute video (provided on CD ROM) that shows how to run a successful strategic retreat.

Neville has also made a series of videos on strategic planning, business improvement, and customer service. Some of these are full-length features, and some can be viewed online through his Web site.

Neville is also a powerful, entertaining and informative speaker. Blending facts with examples, stories with case studies and ideas with implementation strategies, he delivers profound messages with a light touch.

Neville has been featured in a BBC documentary, spoken on radio, been quoted in the press, has made a series of videos, and has written many articles.

Please visit Neville at www.lakegroup.com.au.

Kristin Hickey has a Bachelor of Arts (Honours) degree from the University of Otago and a Masters of Business Administration from Bond University (Queensland). Kristin's particular area of expertise is Customer Service and Service Quality.

Kristin lectured at Bond University for five years in Marketing and Management and then moved into market research, where she has spent the past five years working with clients such as Telstra, Toyota, KFC, Pizza Hut, George Weston Foods, Microsoft, Thorn and Johnson & Johnson. Kristin's work extends over both qualitative and quantitative research, including advanced modelling, new idea generation, strategic marketing plans and marketing implementation strategies.

Kristin now co-directs the latest venture within The Leading Edge Consulting Group: a business called FIREDANCE that delivers integrated marketing consulting services, bringing the best analytical and creative thinking together to create powerful marketing movements. FIREDANCE fulfils a strong client need in the Australian market and works closely with the UK consulting firm New Solutions.

Kristin's experience has enabled her to develop a holistic view not only of customer service, but also of business generally. This perspective has been used to help numerous clients make significant breakthroughs. The design and deployment of these breakthrough strategies is Kristin's passion in her professional life.

Please feel free to contact Kristin at kristinh@fire-dance.com.au.

Preface

What do you think about when you hear the words 'customer service'?

Maybe you picture a smiling face behind a counter, or an earnest clerk trying to resolve a complaint, or perhaps an operator taking an order at the other end of the phone. If this is your image of service then you are right – and you are also wrong.

These are all examples of customer interactions, which are only a small part of what customer service is all about. True customer service is much larger.

Customer service is about building an organisation that is appealing to the kinds of customers that you want; it is about giving those customers the experiences that make them come back; it is about measuring and improving what you do and how you do it; and it is about applying sound management principles to all the parts of your business that touch the customer.

Customer service begins before a customer approaches your organisation, and persists after they have left.

Once you understand the full size and scope of what customer service means, all the components suddenly make sense. With this view of customer service it is easy to improve customer satisfaction while at the same time reducing costs.

This book is different from all the others on customer service. Rather than focus on narrow elements, this book provides a total framework that shows you how to prepare, manage and change your business so that you can get the most out of your customer relationships through customer service. The book covers eight key elements:

- understanding customers;
- developing a service strategy;
- delivering service through people;
- creating a service culture;

- complaints management;
- delivering service through processes and infrastructure;
- location and premises;
- measuring service standards, customer satisfaction and loyalty.

This book focuses on external customers, with a particular emphasis on the private sector. However, many of the same principles apply to the public sector and to internal customers.

By the time you have completed this book you will be able to design, develop and implement a total customer service approach. You will be able to make customer service happen in your organisation.

Acknowledgements

A lot of work goes into a book like this. So many people have shared a story, offered an idea or supplied a couple of words of encouragement. It is hard to single out these people, for fear that those omitted may take offence. However, a special mention must go to the following.

Thanks are due to the people at Kogan Page, who have exemplified good service themselves, and who have gone through the intricate and involved process of turning thousands of words and tens of charts into the book that you have in your hands. A special thank you goes to Pauline Goodwin, who initiated and oversaw the process; Jon Finch, who took the book through the editorial steps; and Andy Young and Martha Fumagalli, who invested their enthusiasm in marketing it across the world.

Very special thanks to the people at Housley Communication – and in particular those in the stream-learning division – who worked with us to make the accompanying CD ROM. This is a task that involves not just the filming, but also many, many hours of refining and editing. Thank you Roy Stanton for your hard work and dedication to your craft, and thank you Trevor Housley for the generous use of your resources.

Thank you also to Charmaine Bourke for contributing research and ideas about the people side of customer service. Kristin's thanks must also be extended to The Leading Edge – it is only through being part of a inspirational company that one can truly recognise the difference service excellence can make. Thanks too, of course, to Jac for providing endless support and patience.

No acknowledgement would be complete without once again giving a very large and special thank you to Gayle Lake, who has helped in so many practical ways with research and editing the manuscripts, and who has also given so much indefinable but essential support to help the writers and the writing process. Our thanks and our love (well, actually, Kristin's thanks and Neville's love).

1 Getting into your customers' heads, and winning their hearts

Carl was only 28 when he opened Milsons nightclub. Within three years it was a roaring success, and young clubbers voted it as one of the best after-dark venues in the city.

Now something was wrong. Turnover was tumbling, profits were plummeting, and the enthusiasm for Milsons seemed to have evaporated.

Carl noticed that many of his Friday and Saturday night regulars were queuing up outside the newly renovated Reds Bar in the adjacent street. So, what was going on over there that was so attractive to his customers?

Carl decided to do some research and so he visited the rival venue the following Friday. He had expected some major differences, but he was surprised to find that the Reds Bar was much the same as Milsons. All he could see was that the Reds Bar had a separate area for table tennis and video games, and they served potato crisps at the bar.

As far as Carl was concerned, if that was what the customers wanted, then that is what the customers would get. He quickly installed a table tennis table and several video games and began serving bite-sized nibbles to his patrons.

Despite the investment, the regulars never returned, and the total number of patrons continued to decline. Within a further six months, Carl was forced to close his business.

Surely Carl had done all that could be expected? He was sensitive to his customers. He quickly recognised that the business had begun to decline. He took steps to understand why, and he did something about it.

So, what happened?

Carl thought that recognising his customers was the same as knowing them, and he believed that sharing the same physical space with them provided him with an insight into what drove their decisions.

He was wrong.

Understanding customers requires more than observing them in action. It is more than knowing their names, where they live, their gender, age or income. Understanding customers means getting to know them at a deeper level.

This chapter explores what understanding customers is really all about. It shows you why you need to understand customers, and what you need to understand about them. In the next chapter you will see how you gain this understanding.

Why you need to understand your customers

If you ask a group of people to list why they need to understand customers, you will fill several whiteboards with reasons. You can fit all these under just two headings: profit and loyalty.

Profit

Profit (or cost minimisation in some organisations) is the consequence of:

- concentrating your resources on delivering those outcomes and experiences that your customers value the most, at
- the lowest costs to your organisation, while
- charging the right price.

It is a difficult balancing act to maintain, and is only possible when you have a clear understanding of your customers' perceptions and values.

Loyalty

Loyalty is sometimes seen as a quaint, old-fashioned concept. This is not how it is viewed by those organisations that deliver great service at the lowest cost.

These organisations understand that it is possible to be profitable without a high degree of loyalty, but loyal customers provide the opportunity to make 'super-profit'. This is because loyal customers:

- spread good news about your company – and so recruit new customers;
- cost less to service than new customers;
- spend more;
- keep on coming back.

To generate loyalty you need to go beyond a superficial understanding of your customers – you need an in-depth analysis. For many businesses the effort invested in conducting this analysis is returned many times over. You can gain this level of understanding using the tools and techniques described in this book.

What you need to understand about your customers

Create a list of what you would like to know about your customers. The chances are that it will be a long list. It will include many different kinds of information, such as:

- customer impressions about a particular product/service;
- data about preferences;
- insights about motivations;
- scores that indicate levels of satisfaction;
- and so on.

You could design independent research projects to gather each one of these items of information. However, if all your research projects are developed and conducted separately from each other then you miss the opportunity to integrate the findings and develop a picture over time. You will find it easier to design research and combine the results as well as gain some real insights about your customers if you group your research under the following three headings (note: customer satisfaction is the fourth heading, and this is covered in Chapter 9):

- needs, wants and desires;
- decision-making processes;
- desire for control.

Needs, wants and desires

Once you understand your customers' needs, wants and desires, you will be in a position to provide them with better service, and ultimately secure their loyalty. You will also be able to allocate your available resources in a way that gives you the greatest return possible.

Needs

Needs are the fundamental expectations. They set the minimum level of performance for your business. Customers have **rational needs** as well as **emotional needs**.

Rational needs

Rational needs are the objective requirements for the service to fulfil its function.

Jayne and Phil found their ideal home. Now all they needed was a new home loan to be able to afford it. After visiting banks and mortgage houses, Jayne and Phil had a lot of information. Too much information. The whole 'home loan search process' was turning out to be no fun at all.

Being systematic people, the couple sat down and made a list of the criteria to determine their choice of the right home loan. Here is the list that Jayne and Phil made (how does it compare to yours?):

- low interest rate;
- flexible repayment conditions;
- amount of deposit required;
- low application fee;
- offset account;
- accuracy of recording transactions;
- easy access.

Jayne and Phil were thrilled to discover that one of the loans on their list outperformed all the others on every single one of these criteria.

So, you would expect Jayne and Phil to choose the provider that meets all these criteria, buy their home, and live happily ever after. That would be the rational thing to do. It is not what Jayne and Phil did.

These rational people threw out their considered approach, and chose another provider. This may seem illogical, which, of course, it is. Rational people do not always behave rationally. It is part of the economic models and social truths that define and describe human behaviour. Rational needs form only part of the picture. If you only appeal to rational needs then you are going to miss out on a lot of business. You need to appeal to the other (and often much more powerful) decision driver as well: the *emotional needs*.

Emotional needs

Emotional needs appeal to customers at a much deeper level. They often have more to do with the 'brand' (and what it implies) than the actual service.

To illustrate emotional needs, consider two of the options Jayne and Phil had in their final choice set (names have been changed), shown in Table 1.1.

Table 1.1   Needs met by different providers

Shonky Mortgage Brokers Ltd	Life and Security Banking Group
5.25% interest – conditions apply	6.25% interest – no conditions
No penalty for early repayment after year 9	Flexible repayment conditions
5% deposit required – conditions apply	10% deposit required
£400 application fee	£600 application fee; £400 for existing customers
Offset account	Offset account
Telephone banking; monthly statements	Internet and telephone banking
New market entrant – 12 months in market	*Established banking group for 75 years*
CEO from mobile telecommunications background	*CEO from banking and finance*
Found in Yellow Pages *and newspaper (no other advertising)*	*Major television advertiser, promoting theme of family security*
No sponsorships, brand reputation or banking products	*Sponsor of children's welfare in local community*
	Children's banking products

The rational needs were fully delivered to by the first option – Shonky Mortgage Brokers Ltd – but not the emotional needs. The emotional needs (listed in italics) were pulling the strings. These needs were never fully articulated by the couple, but they tipped the balance in favour of the Life and Security Banking Group.

They were:

- sense of security;
- sense of trust and confidence;
- desire to be associated with the service provider;
- sense that everything will be legal and ethical;
- confidence that the bank will take care of them and their family over time.

So, you need to make sure that your customers' emotional needs support their rational choice to use your business. There are many theories and approaches to help you analyse the emotional needs of your customers. An old favourite – Maslow's hierarchy of needs – has been used extensively, and has survived the test of time.

Maslow discovered that human needs range from primal needs at the lower level, to the more esoteric needs at the higher level. These needs are organised hierarchically – that is, higher-order needs only become relevant once the lower-order needs have been fulfilled. There are three levels in Maslow's hierarchy:

- physiological – survival, safety and security;
- psychological – belonging and social needs (including esteem);
- intellectual/spiritual – self-actualisation.

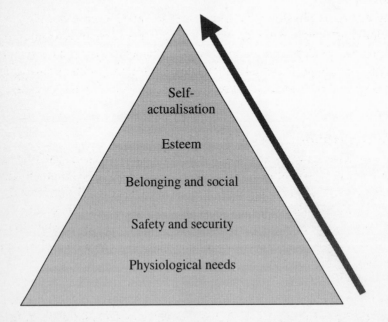

Figure 1.1 Maslow's hierarchy of needs

Physiological needs

At the bottom of the pyramid are the basic needs that support survival. They include the basic 'stuff of life' such as food, water, sleep – and when there is enough of these, sex is important (for procreation). These needs must be fulfilled before people will begin to search for any of the higher-level needs. For anyone who has travelled to Third World countries where starvation and disease are rife, this will certainly ring true.

Safety and security

Once people have fulfilled their primal survival needs, they look for the next level, which includes security, shelter and protection. People express this need by finding a place to live that provides shelter from the elements, by securing a means of income and protecting their health.

Belonging and social

The next level is the need for belonging and close social relationships. People seek to be accepted by their family (or start their own family), form intimate relationships, develop close friendships, or join clubs in an attempt to fulfil these needs.

Esteem

Having met basic physiological needs, and achieved a sense of safety, security and belonging, people will then strive to achieve a sense of esteem, of mastery and reputable standing in the eyes of those considered important. Esteem might be sought through professional achievements, through sporting prowess, cultural achievements, being associated with successful people, dating a supermodel, and so on.

Self-actualisation

As Maslow saw it, the highest level of need was that of self-actualisation. While this term has been commonly confused or misinterpreted by commentators ever since, it basically refers to a level of fulfilment through activities that deliver a true sense of inner contentment. For some, this will be simple activities such as art, sculpture, yoga or writing poetry, while for others it may be climbing Mount Everest, working for a charity organisation or reaching a level of religious spirituality like the Buddhist Nirvana.

So, you are probably asking, how do Maslow's theories affect my business? The simple answer is that customer behaviour follows this hierarchy of needs. In other words, customers will begin by seeking simple, functional needs. Once these are fulfilled, they will begin to seek the higher-level needs – many of which are emotional and significantly deeper or richer. There is every chance that your products/services are meeting higher-order needs. You need to be very clear about what these higher-order needs are, so that you can maximise their value to your customers.

Consider clothing, for example. At the 'opportunity shop' end of the market, customers are more likely to be looking for clothing that provides warmth and comfort (lower-order needs). However, at the 'designer label' end of the market, customers are likely to be fulfilling their 'belonging' or 'esteem' needs. People at this end of the scale will happily pay 1,000 times more for a garment (that offers poorer protection from the elements) than for the opportunity shop equivalent because it has the same label as an outfit worn by an Oscar nominee. When you are appealing to this kind of an emotional need, rational arguments have little force.

With this in mind, take a look at your own spectacular fashion statement. What needs does it satisfy? Consider the pleasure that you got from a special pair of shoes, a leather jacket, an outrageously expensive handbag, a brand name watch, an item of jewellery, a sexy tattoo, or whatever you bought that has a psychological pay-off. There is little that can be categorised as rational in any of these purchases – but the 'feel-good' value is huge.

Now think about your customers. The better you understand your customers' hierarchy of needs, the easier it is to offer the type of service that your customers are seeking. The more you can do that – the more successful you will be.

Let's go back to Jayne and Phil's search for a home loan. They have emotional needs in the following areas:

- Sense of security. (In your business you need to ask: *are we talking to customers in a way that makes them feel safe and secure about their future?*)
- Strong sense of reassurance – this is a big decision, and they want to feel as if they have made the right one. (In your business, ask: *what reassurance cues do we offer?*)
- A sense of belonging and a two-way relationship with the business. (In your business, ask: *are we making customers feel a strong sense of belonging or affinity with us? Do they feel that we care?*)
- A feeling of respect or esteem when dealing with their financial institution. (In your business, ask: *do we make our customers feel special? Do we provide our customers with a sense of self-esteem?*)
- A sense of understanding. (In your business, ask: *do we explain things in a simple, but not in a condescending manner?*)

This home loan example highlights why some financial institutions perform much better than others in an environment where the relative difference in costs (once you expand across a lifetime of mortgage repayments) is negligible.

So what are the emotional needs of customers that you deal with in your industry? Table 1.2 specifies Jayne and Phil's hierarchy.

Table 1.2   Customers' hierarchy of needs (example for home loans)

Level of need	Specific need	Relevant (Y/N)	What is being done to meet this need?
Physiological	Food and water	N	NA
	Sleep	N	NA
	Sex	N	NA
Safety and security	Safety	Y	Banking reputation
	Security	Y	Mortgage insurance; tone and approach
Belonging and social	Belonging	Y	Sense of relationship with the bank through offers of other products and sense of brand affinity
	Social	Y	Bank manager is your friend, not your foe
Esteem	Status	Y	Making long-term customers feel rewarded through tiered reward programmes
Self-actualisation	Self-fulfilment	Y	Enabling individuals to fulfil their goals and dreams

Now, complete the exercise for your own business. Identify which emotional needs your products/services are satisfying on Table 1.3.

(Note: Those of you in the ceramic tile industry who put down 'sex' as a need that is satisfied by your products and service – this is just wishful thinking.)

Be a little creative when identifying the kinds of psychological pay-offs your products and services are providing when you complete this table. Consider the

Table 1.3 A way to analyse the needs met by your organisation

Level of need	Specific need	Relevant (Y/N)	What is being done to meet this need?
Physiological	Food and water		
	Sleep		
	Sex		
Safety and security	Safety		
	Security		
Belonging and social	Belonging		
	Social		
Esteem	Status		
Self-actualisation	Self-fulfilment		

following list, and as an exercise specify a product/service that has provided you with each one of the following:

- attention;
- appreciation;
- dignity;
- respect;
- independence;
- freedom;
- anxiety resolution;
- protection;
- nurturing;
- love;
- a sense of mastery;
- self-respect;
- leadership;
- stability;
- inner harmony;
- control;
- a feeling of being sexy;
- a feeling of being cool;
- a sense of camaraderie;
- an ability to laugh at oneself.

Consider your business in the light of this list, and make sure that you have not overlooked one of the more subtle needs that you are providing to your customers.

Wants

Once needs are taken care of, then wants are the next area to consider. Wants are delivered by competitive businesses. Wants are also both rational and emotional in nature – to meet them means satisfying customers; to fail to meet them generally leaves customers only partly satisfied. In the case of airline travel, wants might include movie entertainment, meal service, complimentary drinks from the bar and hostess service on demand.

Desires

Desires are the 'latent expectations'. They are value-added service components that, once offered a first time, might become a want over time. Some examples of desires include being upgraded from economy to business or first class; new in-flight technology services; extensive menu choice; personalised service or complimentary shuttle service from the airport to the customer's destination.

Figure 1.2 illustrates the hierarchy of customer expectations and how customers are increasingly satisfied as the higher-order levels are met. Note, however, that expectations aren't compensatory, but cumulative in nature. This means that you are still unlikely to 'delight' a customer if you offer them an extensive menu choice but fail to get them to the right destination in reasonable time.

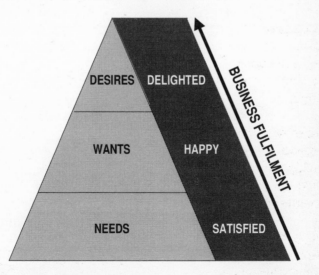

Figure 1.2   How to delight customers

To understand your customers' wants and desires you need to:

- review what you are doing in relation to your competitors and list which elements define the basic level of service (everyone has these), and which elements delight customers (only a few businesses offer these – typically they feature in their advertising as a special attraction);
- review the history of service in your industry and list the elements that have become 'core' and which remain 'value added' over time;
- observe and talk to customers – this research should focus on what they expect as a minimum and what they would value if it were provided (techniques are described in the next chapter);
- determine which elements of service failure cause the most complaints – these are likely to be closer to the customers' core needs than to their latent expectations;
- consider services beyond your immediate industry, as many customer needs are not industry specific (eg the need to answer telephones in a timely and professional manner);
- consider elements of service above and beyond elements that are tangible and costly – eg the benefit of serving customers with a smile.

Now go to worksheet 1 in the Appendix. Here you will find a table that you can use to summarise your customers' needs, wants and desires.

Once these needs, wants and desires are clear, you are faced with a decision. You have to decide the level at which your organisation will perform. Typically, satisfying desires is expensive. Before you commit your organisation to investing this level of resources, you need to consider the strategic position your organisation will occupy. This is covered in Chapter 3.

Decision-making processes

The better you understand how your customers make decisions, the easier it is to help them to choose your business over others. While there are several models about customer decision-making, they all have the same basic four steps shown in Figure 1.3.

Your customers progress through each of these steps every time they buy a product/service. Since you want your customers to choose your business, you need to provide them with what they need at every step, but particularly at the step that is *most critical to them*.

Decision Process	What you need to know	What you need to do
Information search	Information sources and awareness Depth vs breadth of search Attributes for reducing choice set	Create awareness Provide appropriate information
Evaluation of alternatives	Criteria for evaluation Depth and breadth Opportunities to influence	Promise benefits that are important to customers
Purchase	Key influences on decisions Who is the decision maker? What are their needs and expectations?	Appeal to the decision maker Ensure we meet their needs and surpass service expectations
Evaluation	Degree of satisfaction/dissatisfaction What turned them on/drove them away Likely behaviour	Ensure customers are fully satisfied, and fix areas that are letting them down

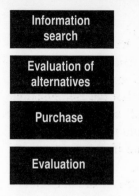

Figure 1.3   The decision process

For example, consider a business traveller who flies regularly between London and Edinburgh. This customer is likely to be a member of a frequent flyer programme and, consequently, might have an extremely rapid decision-making process – simply involving finding out which flight best suits his or her schedule. The post-purchase evaluation is considerably less likely to influence this customer's likelihood of using the same service provider again in the future. The emphasis for the airline is in limiting the evaluation of alternatives and ensuring that the service delivered meets or surpasses the customer's expectations (so he or she remains loyal).

This is different from the customer who, say, seeks a pest control service. Here, the customer is faced with many options and may engage in various types of formal (phone book) and informal (asking friends) information searches. In this case the information search and post-purchase evaluations will have the greatest impact on future business.

So, where should you direct your attention in your business? Consider the following questions:

- Is your business dependent on attracting large numbers of new customers, maybe because they only need to access your products/services infrequently? (Approach: Emphasise information search)
- Do you have strong competitors that your customers will be tempted to access? (Approach: Emphasise evaluation of alternatives)
- Are customers likely to have difficulty in deciding to use your products/services, perhaps because they are luxury? (Approach: Emphasise purchase decision)

- Do you rely on repeat business/word of mouth advertising? (Approach: Emphasise post-purchase evaluation)

You may think that you know the answers to these questions. However, the chances are that your answers and those provided by your customers will be different. Good observation and informal 'talking' to customers followed by a set of interviews and focus groups (see the next chapter for a description of these techniques) around each of the four questions above will help you to gain an accurate picture.

Now, once you are clear about the right emphasis for your business, go to worksheet 1 in the Appendix for a questionnaire that will identify where you currently stand.

Assuming that you have just completed worksheet 1, you will now have a misshapen diamond shape on a four-quadrant grid. This will show you which aspect of the decision-making process you currently emphasise. Check this against the answers you produced in response to the questions to see where your emphasis should be. If your emphasis is right, then you do not need to make any changes. However, here are four examples that show you how to change your emphasis – if you need to.

Example 1: A business that converts and retains customers, but is not well exposed to potential customers. Possible action plan: increase business aware-ness among potential customers.

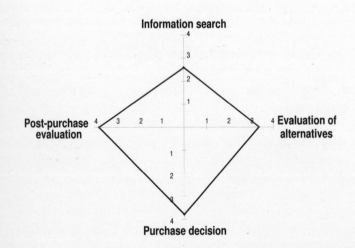

Example 2: A business that is weak in post-purchase evaluation – likely to think it is pleasing customers, but not able to monitor what customers say or do when they exit the business's doors. Possible action plan: develop systems to monitor and follow up with customers.

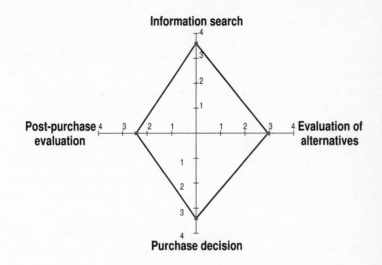

Example 3: A business that attracts the attention of new or potential customers and is good at servicing its current customers. The key weakness is getting potential customers actually to *choose* this business over a competitive offering. Possible action plan: understand what motivates customers and highlight our business's advantage in these areas in communication.

Example 4: A business that is good at getting customers in the door, but does not provide the type of business environment that meets their needs or expectations. Possible action plan: better understand what customers want and deliver service levels that meet or exceed these expectations.

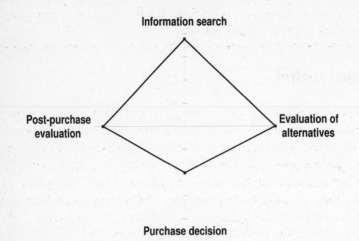

Now that you know which decision step to emphasise, where you stand currently and what you could do to make a change, you can create more favourable customer decisions for your business.

Desire for control

The bottom line is this: customers love to feel as if they are in control of any service interaction or experience. The more control customers believe they have, the more loyal and enthusiastic they will be about your organisation. The customers' desire for control is one of the best-kept secrets among those organisations that achieve superior levels of customer satisfaction. There are four components of control.

Behavioural control

Behavioural control means that the customer is able to do something to modify the likely outcome of the encounter. For instance, a customer in a restaurant can attract attention to ask for assistance at any time.

Cognitive control

This is the control a customer gains from information. Information provides customers with a sense of control through reducing the uncertainty they face and, as a consequence, increasing their probability of receiving a favourable outcome. A passenger on a station is happier to wait when they know how many minutes it will take for the next train to arrive.

Decisional control

This is the sense of control a customer gains from being able to make decisions. Customers like choice – choice conveys a sense of freedom. The key to offering choice, however, is to make sure that a) the choices are not overly complex or extensive (creating information overload), and b) the choice is real in the sense that the options are desirable (a choice between two bad options is no more attractive than a single bad option). So, ATMs have now been designed to provide customers with a series of simple choices to increase their sense of control and flexibility (note denominations and so on).

The illusion of control

Some organisations can readily provide considerable control to the customer, and still preserve their cost structure and performance levels. However, sometimes letting the customer have control spins out the entire service process. Imagine the potential problems, for instance, in a hotel where customers could check in and out any time they chose, or in a university system that allowed students to select from an unlimited range of subjects.

However, it is not the *actual* degree of control that is important to customers, but the degree to which they *perceive* themselves to have this control. Consequently, you need only create the *illusion* of control to improve the customer's perception of your service. This is not deceiving customers, simply giving them the best experience within the budget available to you. Perceived control can be created in a number of ways, but hinges on a few key organisational inputs.

Staff commitment and demeanour

Pleasant and helpful staff can instantly make a customer feel as if they have some control over the situation or service process. A frontline employee's ability to accept responsibility, listen empathically to the customer and to provide immediate solutions help the customer to feel that they are driving the service interaction and outcome (see Chapter 5).

Willingness to modify organisational layout or processes

Subtle layout or process changes can often have dramatic impacts on a customer's sense of behavioural, cognitive and decisional control. Take, for instance, some simple, yet effective changes to an incoming customs' process at an international airport. With little impact on staffing or operational costs, the following changes were implemented to improve customer flow and satisfaction:

- 'Express' queues were instituted for incoming passengers with native passports or whose arrival cards have been pre-processed at the other end.
- Queues were separated according to expected delays (countries of higher risk) to minimise lengthy wait times for the majority of travellers.
- A dedicated staff member reviewed the immigration cards of travellers while they were queuing, to minimise any delays created by incomplete cards at the counter.
- A snake queuing systems was used to reduce the perceived length of the queue in busy periods.
- Friendly and helpful staff were available to help complete immigration cards, answer questions, or simply show empathy to customers experiencing delays.
- Reassurance was provided to incoming passengers that family, friends and business colleagues awaiting their arrival had been duly advised of any expected delays.

Willingness to listen to customers

While the importance of willingness to listen to customers seems obvious, it is important to recognise the degree to which effective listening can lend itself to creating perceptions of control. The car owner with little mechanical expertise will feel uncomfortable if his or her lay description of the car's mechanical problems is dismissed by the mechanic on the job. It is a fact of human nature that we all like to be heard – we like to have our say and be listened to willingly and without judgement. This not only makes the customer feel better about the service, but can often create a competitive advantage.

Now, use the 'observation' and 'talking' techniques (described in the next chapter) to investigate these three components that deliver the illusion of control.

Once you have completed your research, go to worksheet 2 in the Appendix. The chances are that when you have completed this worksheet you will find some easy ways to improve the way your customers perceive your organisation.

Introducing control

You need to do what you can to give customers control. In worksheet 3 (in the Appendix) there is a simple table. Use this table to highlight the amount of control you currently offer your customers, and to identify where you could introduce more control (again, find this information through observation, talking, experiencing, interviews and focus groups – as described in Chapter 2). If there are ways to increase customer control that would be easy for you accomplish – then do it.

So, there are your customers. Irrational, driven by emotional needs, sensitive in their decision making, all bringing their own set of needs, wants and desires, all looking for some degree of control. Bless them.

Now that you have got into their heads and hearts, you need to gather the facts that will enable you to deliver the right kind of service. This is covered in the next chapter.

2 Getting the facts through straightforward research

If there is one constant about customers, it's that they will change – in taste, in attitude, and in demands. So we will continue to learn. Continue to think like a customer and find new ways to give them the best possible experience. . .

Charlie Bell, CEO of McDonald's, Australia

The better you understand your customers, the easier it is to provide the aspects of your products/services that deliver the greatest value, while at the same time containing your costs.

There is a lot to understand. As we have seen in the previous chapter, you need to understand what aspects of the decision-making process animate your customers, you need to tune into their needs, wants and desires, and you have to do what you can to provide control. You will also want to test specific ideas, and find out about specific issues. This means you have to do a lot of research.

There is a misconception that because customers are complex, learning about them is an extremely costly exercise. This is not true. There are a variety of ways you can learn about your customers, many of which are within the financial scope of even very small businesses. In this chapter, we will look at a variety of techniques – from the cheapest to the most expensive.

Observation

Observation is straightforward and powerful, and yields a remarkable amount of information. It simply involves observing customer behaviour (as the name

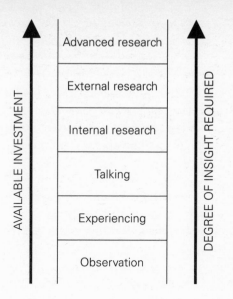

Figure 2.1   The types of research

implies). This type of research can be conducted by almost anyone in your organisation, from a junior employee through to senior management.

The first use of observation research is to reveal basic patterns of customer behaviour. Observing supermarket customers, for instance, is invaluable if you are designing a new store layout, as customers tend to follow consistent patterns of movement – even though they are free to go anywhere. Observation research is also able to reveal where people look (shelf placement strategy), what cues they follow (promotions or point of sale strategy), as well as points of hesitation or uncertainty (information/communication strategy).

The second use of observation research is to give middle and senior managers the chance to learn about the many subtle activities that make up the service interactions, and the interplay of these elements. A report about the number of complaints does not live in the memory in the same way as a red-faced customer who clearly feels that he or she has been ill-treated.

Think about your organisation. Where do queues form, where do the large volumes of calls arrive, where do customers form initial impressions? Get out of your corporate suit (if you wear one), dress like your frontline people and then go to those places and find a spot where you can be reasonably unobtrusive and quietly observe what is going on.

Look at the faces of the customers to see when they register surprise, frustration, pleasure, and so on. Note whether there are common experiences that seem to drive those reactions. Now look at your frontline employees. Note what they find difficult and easy, what they do to provide service, how long it takes, and what reactions they produce.

A few hours of observation will provide you with amazingly rich information. If you have not observed your customer contact people for a while, you will definitely be in for a surprise of some kind – guaranteed.

Experiencing

OK, so experiencing is not, technically, a type of research. Nonetheless, experiencing your service from a customer's perspective is a simple and extremely revealing exercise.

Experiencing involves management putting themselves in the customer's shoes for a period of time. Too often management become so intimately involved in the working of the business that they forget what it is like to be a customer. Similarly, employees can go through their whole career without knowing what it is like to be on the other side of the counter.

So, what would you have to do to experience your organisation from the customer's point of view? Try ringing in with an enquiry (if you must, you can put on your favourite fake accent), try accessing a service, or try making a complaint. Be careful to note every step of your experience so that you can make the necessary changes later on. Try, too, to encourage your employees to engage in these exercises – a mountain of understanding can repay a little investment of time.

Talking

Talking is something so simple that it often becomes overlooked or underrated by organisations. So, who should you be talking to? There are two groups: customers and employees.

Customers

You can learn so much by asking customers good questions and then being quiet and listening to the answers. Such discussions need not be formalised research projects. A maître d', for instance, can learn an awful lot about his or her customers simply by moving around the restaurant tables. A mechanic can better understand his or her customers by investing more time at either end of the service process. A shopkeeper can ask questions to discover what customers really value.

Next time you are with a customer try asking one, or all, of these questions:

- What one thing could we do differently next time?
- What was the best part of your experience with us today?
- What changes would you make if this were your business?

Be careful to listen objectively. Some golden rules for listening include:

- Avoid becoming defensive – listen to the problem rather than trying to find an excuse.
- Avoid attributing blame – listen to what is being said rather than trying to point a finger.
- Provide encouragement to the customer to share information honestly and openly.
- Encourage the customer to express emotions as well as relate facts – this will help you understand how your customers *feel* about your organisation.

Once you are comfortable collecting information from customers, you will probably want to progress to gathering deeper and more interesting insights through 'in-depth interviews'. As the name implies, these are lengthy one-on-one discussions to gain a qualitative understanding of customers' wants, needs and perceptions of your business. These interview sessions can be conducted in almost any environment – in the individual's home, at work, or even jogging with time-poor senior executives. Generally the interviews would extend between 30 and 90 minutes, depending on the depth of insight required (and, if you're jogging, your stamina).

A form of in-depth interview is 'accompanied shopping'. In the accompanied shop you get to take the customer shopping. Say, for instance, you owned a health food store and were interested in *how* customers searched for and chose their vitamin supplements. Having picked the right kinds of people to favour with this experience (see later in this chapter), you should meet them first and ask them general questions about their attitudes towards vitamins. You might have this discussion at a mutually convenient location, or on the way to a health food outlet, chemist or vitamin store. The types of questions include:

- Where do they normally shop for vitamin supplements?
- Why do they shop there?
- What is the difference if they buy them elsewhere?
- What do they look for in vitamin supplements?
- What cues are they after?
- What types of vitamins are they looking for and why?
- What is the role of service assistance and advice?
- What about the reputation of the store?
- Are they affected by shelf placement?
- What is the impact of price?
- Are they impressed by brands?

When you go into the store with them, stop asking questions and observe. Watch to see what the customer is looking at and what catches their eye. What part of the store do they immediately seek out? What shelves do they consider first?

The objective of the accompanied shop is to remain relatively unobtrusive to minimise your influence on the customer's behaviour. Observe their interactions with the products as well as with the people, signage in the store, and so on. Note what questions they ask, what advice they are seeking, where their concerns lie. Note also where price fits into the whole picture – are they choosing between products in a particular price range, or are they considering all options? Compare what they actually do with what they said they would do.

Take the customer to several stores one after the other and ask them questions before and after each service encounter. This will enable you to gain a good perspective of what is important at the product level and store level as well as the service level. A good example of this was a study (that we had the fortune to be involved in) of how beer drinkers chose what beer to drink as they entered a pub. The research provided us insights with memorable evidence that focus groups could not possibly provide. The fact that we had to enjoy cold beer at each establishment was, of course, all in the name of science and entirely incidental to the study.

Employees

As well as talking to customers, you should also talk to your employees – particularly those on the front line.

Think of an iceberg. Just as almost 90 per cent of any iceberg is hidden below the waterline, so management is often blind to 90 per cent of the core problems in customer service.

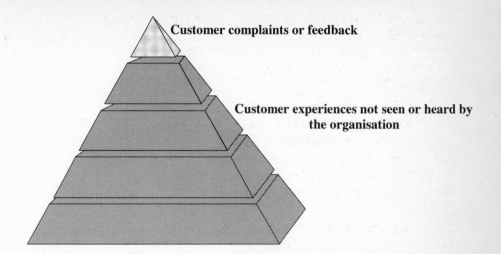

Customer complaints or feedback

Customer experiences not seen or heard by the organisation

Figure 2.2   You cannot see most of your problems

Frontline employees interact directly with customers on a day-to-day basis. They are closest to the customer and most likely to know what the customers like and dislike about the service. They are the first to suffer the wrath of customers when something goes wrong, and see the smiles of pleasure when the service 'hits the spot'. Consequently, they can provide useful feedback on how to improve service processes, or recover from service mistakes.

There are two straightforward ways to gain good frontline data from staff. The first is to talk to them individually. Simply take a tour around the frontline positions and ask questions like:

- What is your greatest frustration at the moment?
- What seems to be the greatest frustration the customers are having at the moment?
- What do you think we could do to fix these frustrations?
- What do the customers seem to like the most?
- What could I do to make your job easier?

Be careful not to be defensive when you ask these questions (if you are, then people will quickly work out that you do not really want the truth – and they won't give it to you). Also, make sure that you let people know when you have made changes based on what they have told you.

The second way is to have small group discussions. These are not necessarily fully developed focus groups (although they can be) and should be relatively informal groups of five to eight people, perhaps over a sandwich lunch. You can ask much the same questions that you asked individuals, but this time you can see people's reactions to what others say, and you help the group to build on ideas.

There is a considerable amount of information about your organisation – and your customers – that resides in the heads of the front line. It is information that is never captured in any formal system. If you can unlock just a fraction of this, you will be in a position to provide considerably better service, probably at a significantly reduced cost.

Internal research – qualitative

There are two types of internal research: qualitative and quantitative. Qualitative research explores customer sentiment, attitudes, values or behaviours – typically in focus groups or one-on-one interviews. In qualitative research you are looking to uncover a 'truth' that was previously unknown.

Quantitative research involves collecting answers to predetermined questions (usually by a survey) from larger numbers of respondents. In quantitative research you are finding out how many people agree with something that you suspect to be true (because you found out about it in the qualitative stage) or how many customers like/dislike something your business is doing.

This section deals with qualitative research, in particular the focus group. Before you rush out and start conducting focus groups, you need to be sure that they will be more beneficial than in-depth interviews (which were covered in the previous section). To choose which one you should use, consider Table 2.1.

Focus groups

The use of focus groups is a key technique, perhaps *the* key technique for gathering facts about customers. It is hard to be serious about customer service without including the focus group in all kinds of situations to collect information. However, it is important to realise that running a focus group is not as easy as it sounds. Most professional qualitative researchers have had years of training and practice to hone their skills – skills that range from communication techniques (verbal and non-verbal) through to advanced understanding of customer psychology.

Table 2.1 Choosing between in-depth interviews and focus groups

Advantages of in-depth interviews	Advantages of focus groups
Greater depth of insight gained from each individual (if individuals are selected to represent the population of interest, relevant generalisations can be made)	Fewer sessions are required, as each group will reveal breadth of insight where individual differences are highlighted
Better for 'sensitive' topics where customers may be reluctant to share information in front of others (ie medical conditions, personal finance)	Discussion is generated that often extends customers beyond their normal scope of thinking and highlights where differences lie
Flexibility of situation	More cost-effective way of gaining 'simple' insight from customers
Ability to gain observational insight about the customer at the same time (ie 'in situ' interviews – in the person's home; at a bar or restaurant, etc)	Sometimes, if enough groups are conducted, the qualitative research can be quasi-quantitative in nature
Ensured focus and attention of respondents	

In this book we have provided you with the building blocks you need to design a successful focus group, along with an understanding of the fundamentals of focus group moderation. On the accompanying CD ROM, you get the opportunity to see a focus group in action. You should watch this example before you run a focus group of your own.

There are seven key dimensions of a successful focus group:

- recruitment;
- relaxation;
- listening;
- managing;
- probing;
- the use of specific techniques;
- interpretation.

Recruitment

Recruitment of a group is one of the key determinants of group effectiveness. Keep in mind that the *effectiveness* of the groups depends on the degree to which customers feel relaxed, comfortable and trusting. To achieve this you need to:

- Recruit groups of customers who are *relevant*. In the example of Carl and his nightclub (whom we met at the beginning of the previous chapter), Carl is interested in people who regularly visit inner-city nightclubs, so it might be unsuitable to recruit anyone younger than 16 or older than 50.
- Recruit customers who are *representative* of the population of interest. If you are talking to customers about cars, for instance, you want to make sure you talk to a group broader than drivers of just one make of car. Try to avoid customers who might reflect extreme opinions, as you are trying to capture commonly shared views.
- Recruit groups of customers who are relatively *homogeneous* in terms of their attitudes and opinions so that each member of the group feels comfortable sharing their ideas and opinions. So, if you are examining attitudes about banking, you might talk to young adults separately from family heads; if you were talking about beer and were interested in both male and female drinkers, you would generally separate the groups because of product-based concerns (size of vessel, calories) and image differences (how the image reflects on them). This becomes even more important when you are discussing areas of a sensitive nature (eg financial investments).

While it is easier to talk to customers you know or like, it is more important to get an unbiased view and – if possible – gain a perspective of your competitors at the same time. Write down all your requirements on a sheet of paper. These are the 'recruitment specifications', defining who you want to speak to in each group. An example is shown in Table 2.2 for Carl's nightclub.

Here you can see the groups that Carl needs to understand better. The rationale for each of the groups is illustrated in the final box in each column.

Once the groups are clear, the next step is to use these criteria to construct a set of questions to make sure that potential focus group participants fall into one of the chosen categories. So, when Carl recruits his respondents, he can read through the list of questions to see if they 'qualify' for any of the four groups. If they do, he can ask them to attend a focus group at a particular time and location; if not, he can thank them for their time and ask whether he can record their name and details for possible research in the future.

Table 2.2   Carl's recruitment specifications

	Group 1	Group 2	Group 3	Group 4
Demographics	Single males aged 18–24	Single females aged 18–24	Professional males and females aged 25–35	Males/females aged 20–30
Behaviours, interests and attitudes	Visit clubs at least once a week, interested in new clubs/ experiences	Visit clubs at least once a week, interested in new clubs/ experiences	Less frequent club visitors, but spend more when they do go out	Club loyalists (4 from Milsons; 4 from Reds Bar)
Other	Like to be seen as 'trendy'	Like to be seen as 'trendy'	Prefer more sophisticated environments	High visitation of 'favourite' club over past 3 months
Recruitment objective	*Understanding opinion leaders in the nightclub market*	*Splitting females from males to avoid 'flirtatious' interactions in groups*	*To determine how the needs of this group differ based on age and income*	*'Conflict' group designed to explore drivers of club preference and loyalty*

Typically, a focus group has between six and eight people. In order to actually get to talk with this number, you need to assume that some people who agreed to participate, and promised to be at the right place on time, will not show up. Standard practice is to over-recruit (secure nine confirmations to talk to seven or eight people), and ensure that each potential participant is personally called on the day of the group meeting to confirm that they are still coming.

Also, you get better attendance (and participation) when people are aware of the reason for the research (ie to use customer feedback and insights to improve our service to the customer) and this will be better still if they receive something to compensate for their time and effort.

Relaxation
You may think that customers cannot wait to tell you what they think of your current service, and are bursting to articulate their future wants and needs. You

may expect that they have organised their thoughts. You may believe that their confidence will not be shaken when they go into unfamiliar surroundings, to sit with people they have never met before to answer questions posed by a stranger. You may be wrong.

The reality is that you only achieve the quality and depth of input required if the people you speak with are relaxed and comfortable and if they are ready to share their thoughts, ideas and opinions. This does not happen by accident. We have already covered how recruiting similar types of people (or those with similar attitudes) helps to make respondents feel comfortable. Other ways to increase the level of relaxation and trust include:

- Avoid boardrooms or 'formal' environments.
- Have respondents sit on couches or comfortable chairs.
- Serve food and beverages (but avoid alcohol).
- The introduction is critical: try to relax the participants as quickly as possible with your tone, use of first names, etc.
- Ensure that the participants know what is expected of them. Make it clear that it is informal, there are no right or wrong answers, emphasise that their participation is extremely valuable, etc.
- Include an introduction exercise – have everyone introduce themselves and include background information so everyone feels they know one another a little better.
- Allow participants to talk as freely as possible at first – structuring the discussion too early will make them feel pressured.
- Start with light topics – easy to answer and light-hearted.
- Provide positive reinforcement – smile and thank participants for their contributions (even if you don't think they are particularly useful). When you sense that everyone is relaxed, you can control the discussion more deliberately.

Listening

While it seems obvious, the art of listening is critical for effective focus groups. There is a big difference between hearing and listening. Listening means making sure that you collect the information that you really need by asking the right questions and 'hearing' all the information that is communicated. Next time you are listening to a group, pay particular attention to the following:

- Listen to *everyone* – often the loudest or most vocal people provide the least information, while the quietest speak up only when they have some-thing *really* important to say.

- Don't just listen to *what* participants are saying – listen to *how* they are saying it. Over half of the information that people communicate comes through non-verbal cues (some studies say as much as 70% of all inform-ation is communicated non-verbally). If someone says 'It's pretty good', with a shrug, it is likely to mean 'It's very average'. However, a customer who says, 'It's pretty good' with eyes raised, head nodding and lots of animation is telling you that the service is great. Be prepared to challenge what people are saying to get at the truth. If the verbal and non-verbal cues do not match, then you could say something like, 'I hear you saying that you like the service, but you do not look absolutely convinced. What reservations do you have?'
- Don't listen to rubbish. Sometimes people launch into elaborate stories about their service experiences – long boring stories, which tell you little about the issues you are exploring, and which do not help you to meet your research objectives. You need to protect your precious time with the group and firmly steer the topic back to the areas that you need to discuss.
- Resist the urge to interrupt. Once you are on the right topic you need to let the person have their say. If you interrupt, they will lose the flow, their confidence will diminish and other people in the room will be less inclined to make a contribution. Once you begin to interrupt, you will lose the trust of the respondents you have so carefully built up.

Managing

It is your focus group. You have put it together to explore a set of issues. You need to make sure that you get what you want. To do this you need to make sure you are in control of the group. Your ability to retain control will ensure you can ask the questions you need to and you get to hear all the answers. You owe it to yourself, and the people in the focus group expect you to define the areas that will be covered. You need to do the following:

- Quieten noisy people, and bring out the opinions of the quieter partic-ipants. You can do this by what you say, as well as deliberately controlling your own body language. It is amazing what happens when you turn away from one person and invite another to speak by using eye contact. Almost always the first person will finish their sentence and stop talking.
- Make sure you keep to a time-line. You should prepare a discussion guide that allocates the time you wish to spend discussing each area. Here is Carl's plan for his focus groups:
  - Introduction (10 mins)
  - Discussion of general category behaviours (10 mins)

- Discussion of how customers choose one nightclub over another – what considerations come into play and how important each of these considerations is (20 mins)
- What do customers really love about their favourite nightclub? What makes a great nightclub experience? What makes a lousy experience? Which is their least favourite nightclub and why? (20 mins)
- Get customers to close their eyes and imagine their ideal nightclub. What does it look like? Get the respondents to write down all the details on a piece of paper, then discuss. How do they feel in this type of environment? What do they like and dislike? (20 mins)
- What could Milsons in particular do to encourage loyalty? What is the service like and how would they improve it if they were management? (10 mins)
- What image does Milsons currently have as compared with Reds Bar among their friends and wider community? Why is this? (10 mins)

Probing

Probing is a critical and masterful talent of effective moderators. Basically, it relates to the *types of question* and the *way* in which questions are asked. Here are some of the essential clues to effective probing:

- You should probe to understand the emotions or thoughts *behind* the information respondents are giving you. Often, people give you the facts, but you need to understand what is driving their thinking and behaviour.
- Don't let an interesting comment slip by. If the timing is inappropriate (ie someone continues the conversation), make a note of the issue and return to it with follow-up questions.
- These are areas you are genuinely interested in – *show* your interest. Change your voice or intonation to ensure that respondents are aware that this is important feedback they are giving you.
- Start your questions with the phrase, 'What is it that. . .' (eg 'What is it that you like about Milsons?' 'What is it that makes you say/feel like that?', and so on.) Make sure that you avoid the *why* questions – they encourage respondents to say, 'I don't know' and shy away from further answers.
- If respondents offer an 'odd' or unexpected answer, this is a good time to probe. Try to explore how respondents 'feel' – ask them to create a list of words to describe what they are talking about, and then get them to explain what each of the words means in their own terms.

- Plead ignorance. If a customer says something is 'good', then probe: 'In what way is it good?' 'Is everything about it good?' 'How does it make you feel that it is good?' 'What are those feelings about?', and so on.
- Don't accept 'I don't know' for an answer. At some level people do know. Often it is a hint that you have asked the question in a way the respondent finds difficult, and the question may just need rewording.

The use of specific techniques

Probing will help you to clarify what people have said – and why they have said it – but this will not necessarily give you the answers you need to more complex and subtle aspects of the customers' experience. To get this kind of information you need to ask direct questions – indirectly.

Say, for instance, you want to ask about the *image* of your business. One way might be to ask obvious questions about image, such as 'What kind of image do we have?' You will get answers to this question. Rational answers. Answers that are the customers' best attempt to put into words a whole parcel of experiences and feelings that is extremely difficult to articulate. This is probably not what your image really is.

Another way to get at this kind of information is to use 'projective techniques'. Projective techniques are used to transpose the respondent out of their normal thinking habits so that they can gain access to impressions that are stored in a more complex way in the brain.

A really great example of a projective technique is the 'corridor technique' (see your CD ROM). Here, the moderator asks the group to close their eyes and imagine they are walking down a long corridor. At the end of the corridor is a door that has a sign on it. This sign is the name of the business that is the focus of the research (in the continuing example of Carl's nightclub, it is Milsons).

The respondents are then asked to imagine opening that door and walking in to the world of Milsons. Ask them to look around and experience that world: the environment, the activities, the colours, the sounds, what is happening, etc. When they have spent several minutes picturing this world, ask them to walk back through the door and close it behind them before opening their eyes. Using a pen and paper, get the respondents to write down what the world of Milsons is like for them. When they have all completed their written descriptions, get them to read them out one at a time. Probe how they felt about being in that environment, and focus on what they liked – or didn't like – about it.

Some respondents give you rational images (ie crowded nightclub; smoky; loud; people having fun), in which case you can ask them rational questions – what they liked or disliked; did they feel they fitted in? what would they change about it? and so on. Others give you emotional responses that appear to have little to do with the nightclub industry, such as world with trees, outdoor images, cloudy cool weather, animals, quiet music, and so on. These images portray the way those people feel about your business. Ask this group more emotive questions – were the clouds threatening, or refreshing? How did they feel in this environment? In what other places do they feel like this?

If you are interested in the image projected by a competitor, then run the same exercise, but with the door at the end of the corridor being that of a competitive business. You often find some very interesting and much deeper differences than you might if you were using only rational questioning techniques.

Interpretation

Just one focus group will produce a lot of information. If you are running a series then you end up with thousands of separate bits of data. You are going to have to make sense of this, and present your findings in a way that is crisp and leads to action. To do this successfully, you need to interpret your findings along the way; this allows you to form hypotheses and test them as you move through the groups.

A good way to start this interpretative process is to create a 'map'. For example, where do nightclubs fit in their set of possible social activities? How do customers see the different nightclubs – how do they compare them? A two-dimensional axis helps in this mapping process. For instance, you might decide that the most relevant considerations in nightclubs are a) the age of the club's clientele, and b) the degree of variety (music, range of bars, theme nights, etc) offered. Now plot the different offers on the map according to how *customers* see the world. This should give you some insights into how the clubs differ and where the market is heading, by overlaying your findings about what clubbers are looking for (identified by the grey circle in Figure 2.3).

This mapping gives you a richer understanding of where your business might be inadequate in meeting customers' expectations, even if you are providing the best service you possibly can. Remember, customer service is not just about serving customers with a smile – it is about making sure the whole service offering is meeting the needs of your customers. Make lists of all the areas mentioned as affecting your customer service. For Carl's nightclub, this could be:

● music volume;
● fast drink service;
● affordable drinks;

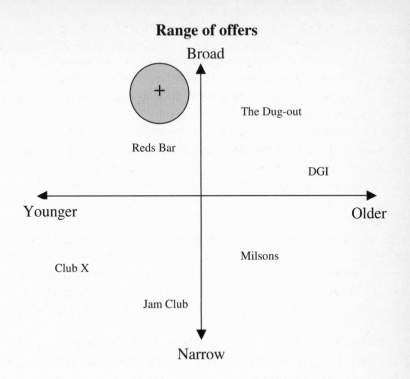

Figure 2.3   An example of a two-dimensional map

- food availability;
- atmosphere;
- attracts interesting people;
- easy to get to, etc.

You may find that you have as many as 40 or more ideas that customers have told you are important. List all these down, then review the list you have. Are any of the ideas overlapping? Are they saying the same thing in a slightly different way? If so, combine them and reduce them into a single category.

Now, reduce the list to a maximum of 25 areas. A straightforward way to do this is to write all the ideas on cards so you can shuffle them around to form smaller groups. This gives you a framework for understanding what needs to be done in each area. One approach is to list the areas and rate (based on your understanding from the focus groups) what you believe are most important to change so you can begin to form priorities for action. The nightclub example is shown in Table 2.3.

Table 2.3 Carl's priorities for action

Factor	Specifics	Performance	Priority	Action
Timeliness	Fast drink service	Good	Low	Maintain current standards
	Fast food service	Average	Medium	Needs improving
Atmosphere	Room temperature	Poor	High	New air-conditioning unit
	Smoke	Poor	High	Investigate smoke-free units or area
	Music volume	Very good	Low	Maintain
	Décor and fittings	Good	Low	Review in 12 months
	Type and variety of music	Average	Medium	Need music with youth appeal
Customers	Well behaved	Very good	Low	No threat currently
	Interesting crowd	Poor	High	Need to attract younger crowd
Accessibility	Easy to get to	Very good	Low	No threat currently
	Easy to get home from	Poor	High	Need to review taxi access options

If you want, these can then be put into a questionnaire designed to measure the various aspects of service in order to provide an ongoing understanding of what needs to be improved.

So, as we have just seen, running a focus group is not as easy as just chatting to a bunch of customers; it requires a far more rigorous approach to selecting the right customers, asking the right questions, moderation, interpretation and analysis skills. However, you can produce incredibly powerful information. If you are going to run the focus groups yourself, be sure to prepare thoroughly so you can get the most value out of the exercise.

When you are familiar with running focus groups, and you are comfortable with the process, you may want to think not just about the process you need to follow, but also about the *type* of focus groups. As you advance in your skills you may want to create more complex interactions by convening different types of groups. Three of the most common kinds of 'speciality' focus groups are as follows.

Affinity groups

In affinity groups the individuals recruited are asked to bring along a friend or partner. By bringing a person they are close to, people are immediately made to feel more comfortable in what can sometimes be a rather awkward environment. The use of this technique is particularly powerful in the following situations:

- Customers are likely to shop or use the category in pairs (eg home loans).
- The audience of interest is a particularly introverted group (eg young teenagers).
- You believe the second person will give a more realistic account of the individual of interest (eg mood swings during pregnancy).

Conflict groups

Conflict groups are focus groups where the participants are specifically recruited to reflect different opinions. When talking about motorcars, for instance, you create the opportunity for a different kind of discussion if half the group are loyal supporters of one brand, while the other half are equally fervent about another. Conflict groups are useful to:

- highlight differences in underlying values, beliefs or perceptions;
- highlight different rational and emotional needs of consumers within the same category;
- understand what motivates customers of a competitor – so you have a better chance of appealing to them.

In recruiting and running conflict groups, you need to prevent a productive discussion from degenerating into a heated argument. You also need to be careful to avoid the *source* of conflict being something highly personal or too emotional. For instance, recruiting individuals from opposing political lobby groups to discuss local politics would be a recipe for disaster, rather than an insightful discussion.

Pyramid groups™

Pyramid groups™ are used when you are testing a new product and/or communication strategy. A pyramid group™ is a focus group that is split into two mini-groups. Each group has its own moderator and is shown a new product, service or advertising idea within the mini-group environment. Once this is discussed, the two groups come back together to allow each mini-group to present the idea they were shown to the other mini-group. The key purpose behind this approach is to understand:

- what customers took out of the product or communication you showed them (often it is something other than what you were trying to convey);
- the language they use to communicate the idea to the other group (what do they emphasise or de-emphasise; what emotional words do they use?);
- the questions asked of the group listening to the explanation (these are likely to reflect the questions customers will have when they hear about your new products or service or when they see your new piece of communication).

Internal research – quantitative

Quantitative research puts numbers and percentages around the kind of data that you have gathered in focus groups. It measures the elements that were uncovered through surveys or questionnaires. While it is relatively simple to design and conduct a survey, it is time consuming and there are a number of traps that need to be avoided. You need to be sure that you have followed the golden rules:

- Make sure that every question explores only one aspect of the service or of the customer. Don't ask, '*How would you rate the friendliness and efficiency of our staff?*' – you might get a poor score and not know whether it is because your staff are friendly, but inefficient, or efficient yet unfriendly – or both. Instead, ask about both elements as separate questions.
- Design questions so that you know how to interpret the score. Ask yourself, 'What would I do with a high/low score on this question?' If there is no obvious action, then you need to rethink why you have included the question. Every answer should compel you to do something.
- Do not have extreme questions of the kind '*I am always extremely satisfied with. . .*' because no one will agree with this (no organisation is that great), and it will distort the findings.
- Make the questions as simple as possible – remember that the average reading age in the UK is at the level of a nine-year-old.
- Use as many 'closed-ended' questions as possible. These are questions that force the customer to respond using a point on a scale rather than writing in whatever they like as an answer. Closed-ended questions are much easier to analyse.
- Do not have too many questions. People quickly get bored. The longer it takes to complete the questionnaire, the more chance you have of getting 'made up' responses towards the end of it. Aim for a questionnaire that can be completed in 10 minutes or less.

- Test the questions before you use them to make sure that what you think a question means is interpreted in the same way by customers.
- Ask the right questions of the right customers. You will probably have different segments (see Chapter 3) and you need to identify what characteristics within those segments you need to gather data about (age, sex, location, and so on).
- Analyse the data so that the key points shine through. You will produce a telephone book of paper as part of the analysis. Do not present this. Instead, develop lists that show the greatest gaps and priorities.
- Develop a report that describes the survey in plain English, with lots of charts and pictures and as few numbers as possible. Remember, a clear chart is worth a thousand words. This report need not be a written document, and should be in a form that will have the most impact on your organisation (a presentation to staff, workshop with senior management, etc).
- Prepare the senior managers in your organisation for the results. This means involving them right from the beginning and making them aware of the implications of high and low scores. Ask them to guess at the results before they arrive – it sharpens their interest when they find out whether their guesses were correct. The last thing you need is a block of data that people find too difficult to handle, or that is overwhelming.
- Act on the information immediately. Identify the top five changes that you need to make as a result of collecting these data – and make them. The greatest enemy of surveys is procrastination and/or developing too many action plans for too many projects, most of which fizzle out because they are all under-resourced.
- Prepare a straightforward summary of the results that you can give to the front line. This should include the findings of the survey, and the actions that your organisation will take as a result. The better those in the front line understand your customers and how you want them to respond, the better they will be at delivering the right customer experience.

You can conduct this survey in a number of different ways. You can:

- send it in the post (but be sure to include a reply-paid envelope);
- give it to customers and ask them to complete it on the spot;
- conduct it over the phone (evenings during the week are the best times to find people at home);
- send it electronically (by e-mail or post it on a Web site).

Essentially, the less contact you have with the recipient, the less likely it is that they will complete the questionnaire. By post you may get a 1–5 per cent return (depending on who you are and the issue). On the phone you may get a 10–20 per cent response rate, but the phone is considerably more expensive. You might get good responses with a questionnaire posted on the Internet, but remember that your sample might end up being skewed to technology-proficient customers.

Finally, be sure you have a sufficient sample size to provide you with meaningful insight. The bigger the sample the better, as it is more likely to represent all the different types of customers you have. If you have a very small sample (say, fewer than 30 responses), you are subject to bias in analysing the results – you might have just happened to speak to 30 dissatisfied customers, when every other customer on your database is very happy with your service.

External research

This is research conducted outside of your organisation. This might include either qualitative or quantitative research and is typically conducted by a market research company with expertise in either or both areas.

Research outside of your company is recommended in the following instances:

- when you want to be sure you are talking to customers as well as non-customers (or customers of competitors);
- when you need large sample sizes to make difficult judgements;
- when you require analysis at an advanced level to understand core motivations that aren't clear to you, or you are searching for highly emotive needs;
- when you need to have information analysed by different types of respondents (eg do light users of my service think about it in the same way as heavy users do?);
- when you don't have the time or inclination to do the research yourself;
- when you wish to set up a robust system for tracking performance over time and want to ensure that the sample and the responses are comparable over time;
- when you are not really sure about what you want to find out, but know you want the business to improve;
- when you need help interpreting and implementing the findings in your business.

Sometimes research will be commissioned to investigate a particular marketing issue of concern, eg Why have customer defections increased? Why is customer loyalty declining in our business or industry? What opportunities exist for new product development? What type of advertising works best for our type of business? These types of projects are referred to as *ad hoc* studies because they are one-off studies that deliver insights into a specific issue of concern.

In other cases, market research is conducted continuously. Customer tracking, for instance, might map customer satisfaction over time, or might monitor whether a firm is gaining or losing market share. This might involve mystery shopping.

While market research can be expensive, large businesses find it invaluable because it provides insights that simple internal research is unable to deliver.

Advanced research

Advanced research has been included as a separate category even though the same market research firms would conduct this type of research. The reason we have chosen to separate advanced research is that the scope of such projects is very different from standard tracking or ad hoc research requirements. A large service company might, for instance, spend upwards of £300,000 once every three or four years on a major piece of customer work, and the results would be used to direct its business over the next three or four years.

Types of studies falling into this category would include studies on customer usage and attitudes across the market; segmentation studies relying on complex techniques and analyses; econometric modelling using sales data or CRM information; or any modelling customer behaviour or decision-making processes using other complex multivariate techniques.

Now that you are familiar with the kinds of information that you need to gather, and the different types of research available, you will be able to pick the right approach for your budget, and the kinds of information that you need to obtain.

However, customer service is not simply about giving customers everything they ask for – that is a fast route to depressed profits and a weak capacity to develop. Customer service is a balance between what the customer needs, wants and desires and what you are prepared to deliver. Getting this balance right is what the next chapter is all about.

3 Making three big decisions, and building your service strategy

'Get out there and delight your customers.'

That has been the mantra of the service revolution.

'Do what it takes to make sure that every customer leaves your organisation with a smile on their face, and a song in their heart.'

That is how the theme parks work, that is what happens in the airline industry, that is what the big hotels achieve.

It is probably not what you need to do in your organisation.

The *highest* possible level of service is very, very expensive. It is worth achieving only if your product/service is so much like your competitor's that there is no other obvious way to become unique in your customers' minds. Then (and only then) should you spend all the money that it takes to make a bold statement through your customer experience.

This does not mean you should deliver *poor* service; no customer deserves that (well, maybe a few politicians could benefit from suffering at the hands of their own departments). Rather, it means having a service strategy that helps you to identify, install and maintain the *right* level of service.

So, what is the right level of service?

This is a deceptively difficult question. The right level of service is when customers experience the level of satisfaction that keeps them coming back, and at the same time you achieve the level of profit that you want. To show you how to achieve this outcome, this chapter covers the following:

- the three key ingredients for designing a service strategy;
- implementing a service strategy;
- using measures to stay on track.

You will find a presentation on this topic in the CD ROM that comes with this book, and if possible you should see this before reading the rest of the chapter.

The three key ingredients for designing a service strategy

Your service strategy lies at the intersection of three features:

- your desired outcomes;
- customer expectations;
- process capability.

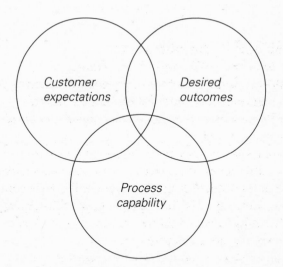

Figure 3.1   The three ingredients for designing a service strategy

There are two key questions for each of these features. Each of these questions drives a set of deliberate choices, and the total of these choices delivers your service strategy.

Your desired outcomes

What is the strategic priority of customer service in your organisation?

Where do you need to be positioned relative to competitors/peer group?

Desired outcomes

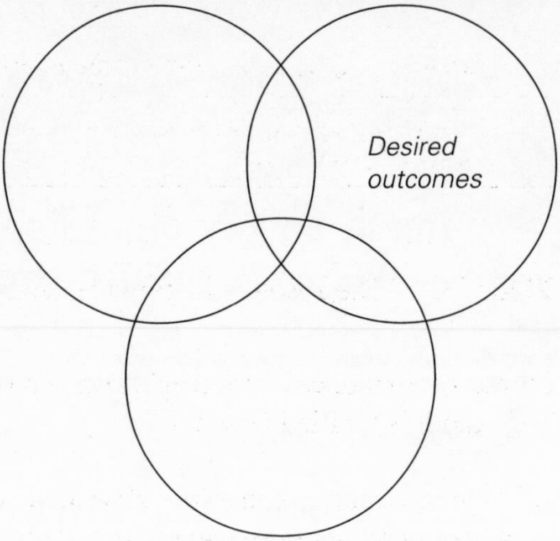

Figure 3.2   Focus on 'desired outcomes'

Customer service is a deliberate choice. To choose the place that your business needs to occupy ask the following two questions:

- What is the strategic priority of customer service in your organisation?
- Where do you need to be positioned relative to competitors/peer group?

What is the strategic priority of customer service in your organisation?

This is a tricky question. Customer service is important to every organisation, but it is not necessarily strategically important. Neville Lake is also the author of *The Strategic Planning Workbook* and you will find articles and online videos (all free) on his Web site that will help you to think about your business from a strategic point of view (visit www.lakegroup.com.au). Once you have reviewed this material, you need to complete two exercises:

- absolute importance analysis (position on a scale);
- relative importance analysis (position compared to other parts of your business).

Absolute importance analysis

Draw a scale that starts at 1, and finishes at 100. It should look like a big ruler.

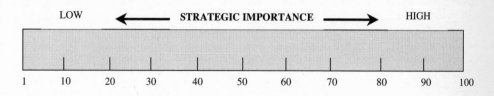

Figure 3.3   The absolute importance analysis

Strategic importance is at the right-hand end of the scale (where the high numbers are), and it is typified when:

- your customer can easily choose to go somewhere else;
- your product is essentially undifferentiated in the customer's mind;
- you have developed a place in the market based on the kind of service you provide.

If these three characteristics are present, then service is all, or at least a large part of, your competitive advantage.

At the other end of the scale (low numbers), the strategic importance of service is low because:

- you are a monopoly, or you have locked in your customers in a way that allows you to behave like a monopoly;
- the product you offer has such a strong brand name that customers will walk over hot coals to get it;
- you have developed strong relationships with your key customers.

Assess where customer service needs to be positioned in your organisation by completing two simple exercises.

First, select a group of organisations that you know enough about to position them on the scale. Choose some that would have low scores, and some with high. Place these organisations on this scale. This is usually really interesting (see Figure 3.4).

Now, place your organisation on this scale, and list the reasons. Think hard about your score. You need to be clear in your mind about the choice you have made – so that you can prompt others to take an objective view.

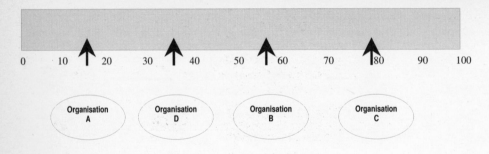

Figure 3.4 Placing organisations on the scale

Now, ask 10–15 key and senior managers to give your organisation a score using the same criteria. You will need to be careful when collecting this data. Customer service is a kind of 'motherhood and apple pie' topic; when you first ask them, everyone will say it is of primary importance. Make people stop and think.

Make it clear that you want to provide not poor service, but the right level of service. A score of 1 is perfectly acceptable if service is not a key strategic driver. Now ask them to rate strategic importance again, and collect their reasons. Add the responses up so that you generate an overall position on the scale. You now have your first piece of information.

Relative importance analysis

List the key processes/areas in your organisation. These will include processing, manufacturing, people management, and so on. Each of these is important – you would not be in business without any one of them – but some are more fundamental to your organisational intent than others.

Convene a small focus group of senior managers and ask them to place in rank order the key processes/areas in your organisation. The easiest way to do this is create a card for each process/area, and ask people to sort these cards. Note where customer service comes on the list. This is your second piece of information.

So, these two exercises give you the information you need in order to decide where you need to place your organisation as a matter of strategic priority. What that actually means you need to provide is answered by the next question.

Where do you need to be positioned, relative to your competitors/peer group?

Positioning is a relative choice. It has to do with how you want to be seen, compared with your competitors/peers. There are three broad levels where you can choose to position your organisation:

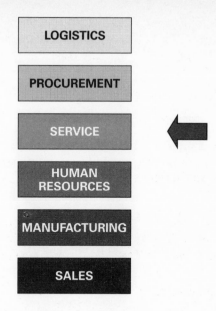

Figure 3.5   Example of a card sort for the relative importance scale

- competitive;
- comparative;
- compliance.

Competitive

At the competitive level you are trying to make a statement about your organisation through the service that you provide. Here you are investing time, effort and money in providing noticeably different levels of service. You need to be convinced that this extra expenditure is repaid with extra business. This is where customer service is pivotal to your business – it is your *key* point of competitive advantage.

Comparative

The comparative level is where most organisations need to be positioned. At this level you are aiming to set your service standards to be more or less the same as those of the others that are your key reference points. In the public sector this means other public-sector organisations, and other large service providers. In the private sector it means matching the key ingredients offered by your closest competitors. This is still a high level of service, but it is no higher than it needs to be.

Compliance

The compliance level is the lowest level of service possible. It seeks to comply with basic standards, but offers little more. It is a level at which some complaints are generated, and where you are unlikely to achieve high levels of customer satisfaction. If you choose to occupy this position you will need to work hard to align your customers' expectations with the levels of service you provide.

Consider your organisation. Where do you need to be?

To answer this, go back to your answers in the first question. In general terms, a score of 85+ on the first exercise means that you need to invest in service because it is a key part of your competitive advantage (competitive). A score of 30–85 suggests that you should match the rest of the pack (comparative), and a score of below 30 means that you should set your service standards to just match median levels for an average workload (compliance).

Consider this along with the level of importance, and modify your decision if you need to. So, if customer service is in your top three, it is likely that it should attract a reasonable portion of your organisation's resources (competitive); if it is positioned 3 to 8, it is still important (comparative); and below that it is probably compliance.

Table 3.1 Summary of decisions

Score on absolute importance analysis	Ranking on relative importance analysis	Competitive, Comparative or Compliance

By looking at these two pieces of information you can judge where you need to be positioned relative to the organisations that your customers would consider to be your peers/competitors.

If you conclude that you need to be at the **competitive** level then you will have to do the following:

- Conduct research that shows which characteristics of the service that you provide have the greatest impact on the customer's perception.

- Identify the level at which you will delight customers on these characteristics.
- Decide how many of these characteristics you will provide at the 'delight' level by looking at your nearest competitor – and going one better.
- Resource your organisation so that this level is achievable.
- Develop service standards and satisfaction measures that contain these characteristics.
- Conduct regular research so that you can be sure that service standards are maintained, and customer satisfaction is sustained.
- Conduct regular research into the level of performance achieved by your competitors – so you can make changes that ensure that you always stay in front.

If you decide that a **comparative** level of service is fine for your organisation then you will need to:

- Identify how your service performance compares with that of your peer group/competitors.
- Set your service standards and satisfaction measures to meet average levels of performance.
- Resource your organisation so that this level is achievable.
- Let your customers know what level of service they should expect.
- Deliver against your promises.

If you decide on a **compliance** level then you need to:

- Be prepared for a level of complaints and dissatisfaction.
- Set service standards and satisfaction expectations that reflect a compliance level.
- Make it clear to your customers what your service standards are, and what expectations they should have of your organisation. Customers may accept that you take two weeks to do what your competitors/peers accomplish in a week – but you have to deliver what you promise.
- Make sure that all the interactions convey an interest in your customers (see the section on 'control' in Chapter 1).

To be able to identify what this really means, you need to know about your customer expectations.

Customer expectations

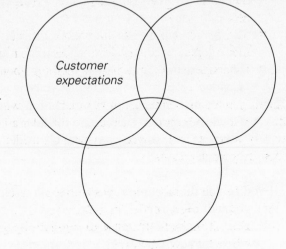

What are your competitors/peer group doing?

What other influences shape your customer expectations?

Figure 3.6   Focus on customer expectations

The two questions are:

- What are your competitors/peer group doing?
- What other influences shape your customer expectations?

To be able to answer these questions properly, you need to examine the different kinds of customers that you have, and determine whether you have any clear segments.

Segmentation

Segmenting customers is useful when you are able to modify your service mix to appeal to different customers. In the airline example, for instance, service providers have effectively developed three separate offers (first class, business class and economy class) as well as a variety of ancillary offers (frequent flyer programmes, airline lounges, and so on). This enables the airlines to maximise their profitability, as customers in these different segments are prepared to pay different prices to fulfil their particular needs.

The best segmentation approaches are those that have the following characteristics:

- Actionable –you can do something different to appeal to the different segments.
- Sustainable – the segments are enduring over time, not just in the short term.
- Simple – the segments are not too difficult to define, so you can readily identify the characteristics of a particular segment.
- Explanatory – they explain something about customer behaviour.

Identify relevant segments in the market in which you operate. Think more broadly than your current customers: consider all customers who might buy the type of products and services you offer. Consider these questions to help you to identify your segments:

- Can you identify the types of people in each segment using key demographics (age, gender, income, etc)?
- Does it make more sense to segment by geographies (where they live, where they work, etc)?
- Do your customers naturally fall into different categories by the types of organisations they work for, or the size of organisation that they come from?
- Are there clear user types based on how they apply or gain benefits from your products/services?
- Is price sensitivity a key way to categorise your customers?
- How might you communicate differently to these different segments?
- Will you modify your offer to appeal to these different groups? If so, how?

These questions cover the key ways in which you could segment your customers. If you have not considered them before, you should organise a meeting of your senior managers and explore each in turn, and its effect and implications for your organisation. The chances are that one or two will be the obvious choices for your business, and you can then develop your strategy – and indeed deliver your service – with these segments in mind.

If you have several segments, then you should consider the following question in relation to each of those segments.

What are your competitors/peer group doing?

Whether you are aiming to match your competitors/peer group or exceed them, you need to know what level of performance they currently maintain.

Before considering the private-sector example, let us examine the public-sector situation. In the public sector there are a group of like organisations that define customer expectations and set the standards that you need to follow. These organisations include other, similar parts of the government machinery. However, in the customer's mind, one big bureaucracy is much like another – so the peer group will also include banks, utilities, insurance companies, and so on.

It is all of these together that should be considered to be the peer group, and it is the median of the service levels achieved that should be the benchmark. In most cases the information can be gained simply by asking the relevant organisations, or you will find that it is published in some way.

If you are in the private sector, you need to look to your close competitors – those who are likely to be doing business with your customers. You will find that there is a remarkable amount of information available about these businesses. You can gain information about service standards and service performance from your customers, from your competitors' Web sites, or from papers that they have delivered at conferences.

You need to develop a list of those organisations that constitute your closest competitors and collect information from the available sources so that you can work out the median level for your industry/peer group.

What other influences shape your customers' expectations?

An examination of your closest competitors enables you to peg your performance against theirs, but in some industries the overall standard is somewhere between very ordinary and poor. This makes all the players in the industry vulnerable to a new entrant that can provide noticeably better service for little/ no extra cost – and win large numbers of customers.

As customers we have a general level of expectations, which we apply to every organisation that we come into contact with. We expect that people will not be rude, that they will not unnecessarily waste our time, that they will provide the product/service on the date that has been promised, and so on. When those organisations that were once known to be at the bottom of the pile for service delivery lift their performance, then this general level is ratcheted up. So, as banks, utilities and telecommunications organisations have made leaps forward, so too have our expectations. These movements form a 'template' against which all organisations are judged.

Therefore, you need to be aware of where the baselines sit, and at what point you may be better than your competition, but still collecting complaints from your customers. Use the techniques described in Chapter 1 to find out what templates your customers use.

So, these two questions tell you about the actual service expectations that your customers have of organisations like yours. Put this information together by following these steps:

- Specify if you need to be competitive/comparative/compliant.
- List key events/interactions that you need to measure, and for each one specify the levels of service performance (with reference to your competitors/ peers) that meet your requirement to be competitive/comparative/compliant.
- Check this level of performance against the other reference points, and if these levels are below commonly accepted standards, then increase your levels to match these standards.
- Create a brief statement to describe your position, accompanied by your performance standards (for more on standards see Chapter 9).

You are now ready to position yourself among your competitors and peers. However, before you do so, you need to know whether or not your processes are able to deliver the outcomes that you want.

Process capability

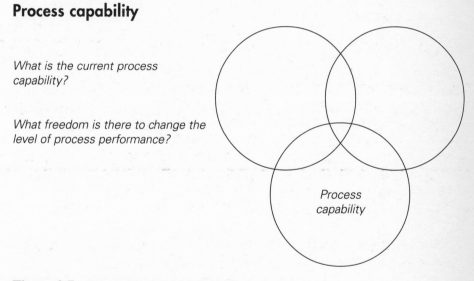

What is the current process capability?

What freedom is there to change the level of process performance?

Process capability

Figure 3.7   Focus on process capability

Process capability is the limiting ingredient. There is little point in developing standards if your staffing levels, resources and budgets cannot sustain the level of process performance required to maintain these standards. The two process questions are:

- What is the current process capability?
- What freedom is there to change the level of process performance?

What is the current process capability?

Many customer service processes are at the mercy of complex variables that produce pronounced peaks and troughs. Simply watch a fast food counter at lunchtime to see how the queue length varies considerably over the hour. A published service for waiting time at a counter needs to be achievable in the face of the longest queue, just as a phone standard needs to be able to withstand the busiest time of the day, or a delivery standard the most crowded route.

Real standards (rather then aspirational ones) need to be developed in the light of process capability, and be adjusted so that they are achievable at peak workloads. This level is relatively easy to assess through process mapping.

Process mapping

There is no shortage of 'work'. Imagine if you were to pick a person off the street, give them a desk and a phone and leave them alone for six months. At the end of this time they would have phone calls to return, meetings to attend, and travel requisitions to go and visit some place out of town. 'Work' grows like weeds. It attaches itself to your processes and it chokes your capacity to deliver outputs, profits and customer service.

To expose this weight of waste (and lost opportunity), first identify five processes that have both the greatest direct impact on your customers, and consume the largest amount of resources. Ask three groups of people to be involved in mapping those processes:

- the customer contact people who spend their days progressing activities through the processes;
- their supervisors;
- the managers of the total process.

Convene three groups and ask them to create a simple map independently, showing how long each process step typically takes. The differences between what people actually do, and what their supervisors/managers think they do, is always surprising. Now, put together a team that will have to invest a number of hours (how many depends on the nature of your processes) developing accurate process maps and then analysing ways to produce the same/better outputs with fewer steps and less cost. As a general guide, processes will be 15–20 per cent dysfunctional within two years of being designed and installed. At the completion of this exercise you will know your true process capability.

What freedom is there to change the level of process performance?

In some organisations an increase in the number of customers translates into an increase in profit, which can then be used to fund an increase in the number of people working on a process. This is not true for every organisation.

Those who are in the public sector typically have set budgets that cannot be varied. If these departments do not collect revenue, then more customers does not mean more money – and so the consequence is a degradation of standards as the volume increases. At the other end of the scale, a very small business may not be able to afford to add a person for a small increase in business, so the existing people have to absorb any extra workload, with the resulting effect on service standards.

If you are in either of these situations then you need to advertise your 'worst-case scenario' levels of service performance.

So, your process strategy is the consequence of deciding where you want to be compared to others, pinpointing what that means for your organisation by examining your customers' expectations and then testing these against the reality of your process capabilities. You need to set your service strategy at the intersection of these three blocks of information. Use Table 3.2 to summarise your answers to the questions, and then create a statement that accurately describes the service strategy that is right for your business.

Table 3.2 Summary table of all key decisions

Issue	Question	Your response	Comment
Your desired outcomes	What is the strategic priority of customer service? Where do you need to be positioned?		
Your customers' expectations	What are your competitors doing? What influences shape their expectations?		
Process capability	What is your current process capacity? What freedom do you have to change this level?		

Taking all the information into consideration, create a straightforward statement that describes your organisation's approach to customer service:

Implementing your service strategy

The table you have just created summarises your strategic approach to customer service. If this is a reflection of what you are doing today and what you plan to do in the future then you simply have to keep on the same path. However, if this table shows you that you need to change your approach to customer service and/ or your level of service delivery then you need to make some important changes in your businesses. If you are in this situation, there are two ingredients that have to be in place. Customer service needs to be strategically important, and there needs to be a way to turn words into action

Making service strategically important

Activities, projects and processes become important when they have a real – and easily recognisable – impact on the bottom line.

In spite of many bold attempts, it is difficult to connect customer service directly with financial performance. Sure, it is possible to calculate the cost of complaints, or to correlate internal indicators (such as organisation culture, performance against standards, and so on) with levels of customer satisfaction. This is really interesting information for fixing processes and problems, but it does not answer the more fundamental question about what opportunities are available to your organisation through initiating service projects/processes that you do not currently have. These are the kinds of data that make CEOs sit up and take notice.

You can develop these kinds of data through three analyses:

- the sub-optimisation analysis (to show financial consequences);
- the market future analysis (to show future impacts);
- frontline feedback (to show day-to-day implications).

The sub-optimisation analysis
In the book *The Third Principle: How to get 20% more out of your business*, Neville Lake shows that most organisations achieve no more than 80 per cent of their potential (OK, so it is an obvious plug, but it is a really good book. If you are nowhere near a bookstore, then have a look at Neville's Web site for some articles: www.lakegroup.com.au). Many achieve considerably less than that. This sub-optimisation is particularly pronounced for customer service.

Just think of your own experiences with frontline people in the organisations that you deal with. How many times could the interaction you experienced have been better? How much of your business has never been captured because the customer contact people would not – or could not – give you the outcome that was possible?

The sub-optimisation analysis is a robust and straightforward way to identify and quantify the distance you need to travel to achieve your own level of optimisation. It shows you what level of performance is possible. It is particularly important when you are building a case for investing in customer service.

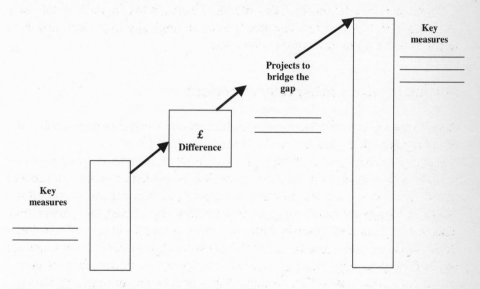

Figure 3.8   The sub-optimisation analysis

Using this framework to <u>analyse customer</u> service, you need to enter the following types of data:

- The tall bar represents the optimised state. This is where your service is as good as it can be within your current cost constraints. This means that every customer contact person takes every opportunity to on-sell, cross-sell, avoid complaints, recover from mistakes, make a good impression, meet a customer need, and so on. This is probably the level at which your very best people are performing, so use these individuals as a benchmark.
- The 'key measures' space next to the tall bar is where you need to record the effect of this level of performance on your organisation's key measures.
- The short bar represents your current performance, expressed as a percentage of the optimised state (most organisations gain no more than 80% of what is possible; many achieve less than 60% and some are below 40%).

- The space next to the short bar is where you record your current perform-ance levels using the measures that you used before.
- The £ box has a space for you to enter your calculations about what the effect on your bottom line would be if the current situation were trans-formed into the optimised state. The figure should show the total of the extra amount you would save through not wasting time and resources, and the extra amount you would make if you were able to take advantage of the available opportunities.
- The 'projects' space is the place for you to identify the kinds of projects that your organisation would need to complete to move from the current to the optimised state.

You should include a number of the senior managers in the thinking that is involved in completing this analysis. You could do this through a set of interviews or in a workshop (set aside about 90 minutes). The reason for their involvement is that you may well produce a big number – a very big number.

If you involve your senior managers in completing this exercise, they are more likely to take it seriously. You will produce some impressive numbers that show what customer service is really worth in your organisation. These numbers are going to show why customer service deserves to be an important part of the strategic planning process.

The market future analysis

The market future analysis is a variation of one of the strategic tools that Neville has described in *The Strategic Planning Workbook*, which is also part of this *Sunday Times* series. You will be using it here to show why customer service is important to your business in the future. The way to achieve this is to analyse where your business is likely to be going, and then show what weight customer service will have in the development of the potential in your business.

The starting point is to acknowledge that a market that used to provide you with lots of healthy profits may no longer hold the same potential. A market that once looked promising may turn out to contain less promise than expected. A market that you had not really considered seriously may offer more than you previously thought.

These changes happen in a way that is not always obvious. This analysis shows you which market is most favourable to your current products/services. You should also consider your potential customers in this analysis, so you can develop a complete picture.

It depends on how well your strategic processes are developed, but if this is the first time that this kind of information has been surfaced in your organisation then it could be that as a result of this analysis, your business may have to face the reality that some changes need to be made. It could be that some of the projects to enter new markets that have started in the past 12 months need to be wound down (a blow to someone's ego). Or perhaps it will become obvious that your business has invested too heavily in industries/customers that are in decline. Or it may be that you need to begin rapidly to convert your potential customers into your actual customers. It is better that your senior managers come to this realisation as a group, rather than you being the bearer of bad news.

So, the first step is to organise a meeting with your senior managers. Before you actually bring them together you need to collect some information, such as:

- profit per (major) customer covering the past two years;
- a list of your potential customers;
- the likely profit you could have made from a potential customer – if they had actually been a customer.

When you convene the group you will need to complete two kinds of analysis: the 'market analysis' and the 'customer service consequence' analysis.

The market analysis
You are going to answer two key questions: 'Where are the market opportunities diminishing?' and 'Where are the market opportunities expanding?'

On the whiteboard draw a simple graph with profit on the vertical axis and time on the horizontal. The time axis should include the past two years and the next three years.

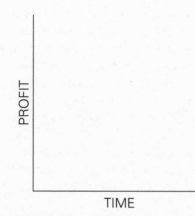

Figure 3.9 Simple profit graph

Explain that you are now going to analyse what is likely to happen in the key markets in the future. Ask the group to review the information that you have collected.

Now, say to the group, *'List all the key markets that you operate in, and those that are possible if you were to gain your potential customers.'* When this list is complete, ask the group to do the following: *'Now, highlight those markets that are really only filled by one customer.'*

If your business does not really operate in markets, but instead has a small number of large customers, then complete the same exercise, using the customers as the focus of your attention.

Break the executive into small groups and allocate each group an equivalent number of markets/customers to work on. Now, ask the executive to sift through the information available, so that they can replicate the picture you drew on the whiteboard on flip chart paper. For each market, draw a line that shows the past two years (fact) and the next three (informed guess). For potential markets/customers they can only show the informed guess. These potential markets should be drawn in green, while the others should be drawn in blue.

Collect up the charts, and stick them to the wall next to each other.

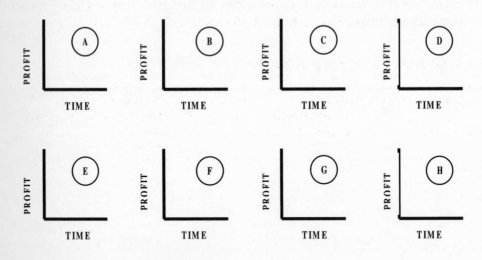

Figure 3.10   The key market analysis

They show you two key items of information. The first comes from the direction of the arrows. If the blue lines are predominantly flat or pointing down then the markets that you currently serve are stable or in decline. Profit in your business will be squeezed. This shows the need for the rapid acquisition and development of new customers, or the development of different pricing/margins. In less than half an hour you could total the sum of the forecasts and show the level of future profit that is likely.

The second piece of information comes from the industries/customers that show the same pattern of arrows. If all the customers of a particular kind, or all the players in the same market are showing a decline in the profit you are expecting, then you need to take a harder look at the attractiveness of continuing to do business with that group.

Using this analysis you can see where the money is likely to come from in the future. And you can now assess the impact that customer service will have on securing the profits that your business needs.

The customer service consequences analysis

The customer service consequences analysis is not so much a formal analysis (although we have given it a name) as a thinking framework to attach additional data to the market future analysis. You will complete this analysis with the same group of managers immediately after you complete the market analysis.

First make a list of those industries and/or customers that you need to be doing business with in the future. Rank-order this list so that the most important appear at the top of the list. Now, create a five-column table (Table 3.3).

Table 3.3   The 'customer consequence' table

Customer/industry	Requires reduced levels of service	Requires the same level of service	Requires an increase in the levels of service	Level of importance

Place your list in the first column. With the group, determine whether each customer will require reduced, the same or increased levels of service in the future (using today's level of service as a benchmark). Place a tick in the right column to signal the decision that is made.

Now, on a scale of 1–10 (with 10 as high), ask the group to estimate how important service will be to your future customers/industries. You will probably find that the majority of those businesses/industries towards the top of the list will require an increase in the level of service, and they will rate it as 7 or above on importance.

You can now see why customer service is critical to your organisation's future success.

Frontline feedback

Those in the front line in your business spend their days interacting with customers. An analysis of frontline productivity is one way to show that a better approach to service will be of value to your business. However, there is an even more powerful strategic reason for understanding and attending to what is happening at the front line – and that is the cumulative effect of frontline behaviour.

The pathway to the future is built on the thousands of little decisions and interactions that happen every day. Your front line are creating your image and reputation with considerably greater force than any advertising campaign, and what they say is so much more powerful than company slogans. An analysis of the kinds of impressions that frontline people imprint on your customers can be a chilling piece of information.

This could be a significant exercise, and if you suspect that there is a problem in this area, you may want to use one or several of the techniques already described in this book.

However, if you just need a quick analysis then use the observation technique. You will need to do the best you can to clear your mind of what you hope and expect the front line will do. Be ready to see and interpret their actions with fresh eyes.

Find a quiet place where you can sit and observe what your frontline people are doing and saying, and make sure that you can see your customers' reactions. Fill in Table 3.4.

Table 3.4 Summary table for frontline observation

Frontline behaviour	Implied message	Customer reaction	Fit with current position on customer service	Fit with future position on customer service

To capture the frontline behaviour successfully you will need to make a list of the standard interactions. It may well contain items such as:

- greeting;
- answering questions;
- providing information;
- demonstrating a product;
- closing a sale;
- handling a complaint.

To assess the implied message you will need to think a lot harder. You will need to assess what the tone, posture, expression as well as the words that are part of your frontline experience all say to the customer. You will probably be able to develop a list after just a few minutes (most people are passably good at interpreting others – even if they are a complete clod when it comes to their own behaviour). Your list may contain items such as:

- I am genuinely interested in you.
- I am not really interested at all, but I am pretending that I am.
- I am not at all interested in you, and I do not care if you know.
- I would be interested in you, but I am very busy and you are taking up my time.
- I wish I could help, but I have no idea what I am doing.
- I really want to talk to my workmate, and you are interrupting.
- And so on.

The fit with current or future position on customer service should be assessed on a scale of 1–10 (with 10 as high).

The chances are that after 15–20 minutes you will have established your list for the first two columns. After an hour or so you will start to see that certain behaviours are repeated, and similar reactions are produced. After a couple of hours you will see patterns, themes and trends. Depending on the kind of business you are, you may find that you are getting low scores on the last columns – particularly if your business needs to do more in the future. This can be a powerful piece of information to fuel the need for change.

Turning words into action

There are four ingredients you need to put in place to make sure that your customer service strategy is successfully implemented:

- Have a clear purpose.
- Have limited objectives.
- Introduce consequences.
- Have an implementation plan.

Have a clear purpose

In his book *Teach Yourself to Think*, Edward de Bono says, '*In my many years of experience in the field teaching thinking I have found that a clear definition of purpose is very rare indeed. This is one of the parts of thinking that people do very badly.*' Make sure that you have a clear purpose for your service strategy based on impact revealed by the sub-optimisation analysis. The clearer the purpose of the changes required, and the more precisely they are articulated in measurable customer contact behaviours and customer outcomes, the easier it is to develop the plan.

So, to use a simple example, instead of saying, 'We want to improve the customer experience on the phone', the purpose needs to specify the following:

- current experience;
- the gaps in the current experience;
- a compelling reason to change – from the frontline point of view;
- the change that is required in terms of specific behaviours and outcomes;
- a way to measure the change;
- consequences for not changing.

Let's now expand on this straightforward example. This is what a business did to cover each of these elements:

Super Utility knew that service was a key element in their capacity to secure business and loyalty. They ran expensive advertising campaigns to reinforce how their friendly and helpful employees would go out of their way to make every customer interaction special.

One day the CEO got a shock. He called into an area (on an outside line) that dealt with many customers, but was not part of the customer service centre. The phone rang out. He tried again, met with an abrupt response, and was immediately transferred to another phone – which rang out. He was furious.

Then he started to wonder. He wondered if this was typical. Had he fallen into the trap of believing his own rhetoric, and had he only seen the statistics from the best-performing parts of the business? He designed some research and asked other executives to join with a number of 'mystery shoppers', and they called the affected parts of the business for the next two weeks.

There was good news and bad news. The bad news was that the CEO's initial experience was about as good as it got – it was in no way untypical. The good news was – well, there wasn't any.

The CEO considered the strategic intent for the business. They needed to perform at a 'competitive' level, and his research showed that this meant a fast response, a friendly greeting and an interest in helping. The purpose for the project that would deliver that level of experience was defined as follows: 'We will improve the customer experience on the phone by answering every call within three rings, ensuring that everyone says "Good morning/afternoon", states their name, and then says "How can I help you?"'

The current experience was documented, and a series of presentations were given to all employees who worked in the areas affected. These were designed so that they contained some humour and some stark facts to show what was wrong with the current situation. People in the room were asked to identify why this was unacceptable, and this information was discussed and tinged with the implied threat that people who behaved in this way were not really the kind of people the business wanted in the longer term.

Then the facilitators of the workshop explained the behaviours that were required. They gave examples, they made people do role-plays and they were absolutely sure that everyone left the room knowing what they were expected to do.

That was not the end of the programme. The mystery shoppers continued to call in. They noted the time it took to answer the phone, and the response they got. After two weeks the results of their findings were discussed with everyone concerned. Clearly, some people had taken the messages to heart, and were behaving in the right way – and just as obviously there were some who had not changed at all.

At the risk of being tedious, the required behaviour – and the reasons for it – were all explained again. This time a consequence was added. The people concerned were divided up into smaller units (of people who sat near to each other). If every person in the unit met the requirements for the next two weeks, then the whole unit would get a bottle of (very nice) champagne. If one person failed, then no one would get the reward.

There is nothing like a little peer pressure to change behaviour – and change it did. By the end of the next two weeks about 25 per cent of the groups won their prize. The offer was repeated for the next two weeks, when over 50 per cent went home with a bottle. The offer was repeated again, and just about everyone was successful this time.

Now the behaviour was so ingrained that incentives were no longer necessary. People kept on answering the phone in three rings, made the greeting, gave their name and offered to help. The mystery shopping continued, and showed that this area had fallen into line with the rest of the business.

Consider any customer service initiative that you have running at the moment. Is the purpose clear and measurable? Is it well defined and controlled? If not, then it is unlikely to deliver the benefits that you want.

Have limited objectives

Colin Powell said that *'The way to win a war is to have limited objectives, and apply overwhelming force.'* The same is true of implementing change.

The biggest and easiest mistake is to try to make all the changes – all at the same time. It is not uncommon to find 25 or more project teams all working to progress equally vital change programmes. After three months people start dropping out because their 'real job' cannot spare them any longer. After six months most will probably have stalled. At the end of twelve months there is a considerable amount of 'blamestorming' (which is where a group of people meet to try to figure out who should be made to seem responsible).

The trick is to pick the six changes that will have the greatest impact, and progress these until they are complete.

Introduce consequences

Someone needs to wake up in the night screaming if things go wrong. The more senior the person, and the harder it is to reallocate the blame, the more likely it is that the project will be progressed. There are three main kinds of consequence:

- cash;
- credibility;
- career impact.

Cash

There is nothing like attaching someone's bonus to the success of a project. Ordinary managers have put in heroic efforts when it is clear that there is a financial reward in the balance.

Credibility

The more closely a person is identified with a project, the more the failure of the project will be seen as a failure of the individual. Most people beyond a certain level do not like to fail – do not like it at all. If someone is seen to own the outcomes, then he or she will work hard to make them happen.

Career impact

The opportunity to manage a strategically important project is the kind of high-profile, 'rung up the ladder' event that people hope for. A success means a good chance at an even bigger challenge; something less can result in a missed opportunity that may have repercussions for years.

Find the person who really needs this to turn out well, and you have found someone who will progress the plan.

Have an implementation plan
Most change fails.

Over 70 per cent of the projects that are designed to create change either fail completely, or deliver significantly less than was promised. If you have identified projects that support your customer service strategy, then these are change projects too and they may well suffer the same fate.

The problem is that most people think that a change process starts with the physical changes, and that a change project can be treated the same as any other project. These are both mistakes.

Employees need to be guided through change by the right team, and they need to be given the opportunity to make psychological adjustments before they are asked to behave differently. To do this they need to believe that the change is important, and that it offers some benefit for them. This takes time and careful planning.

There are six key ingredients that will support service-related change and deliver success. You want your plan to work, so you need to make sure that each is in place. They are:

- a strong mandate;
- a strong purpose;
- preparation;
- the right people;
- early wins;
- communication.

A strong mandate
It is easy for people to sit in a room and make decisions about how to deliberately manage customer service. It is harder to sustain the determination when the first difficulties surface. There will be difficulties; have no doubt about that. There will be the temptation to dilute the projects so that they become faded versions of themselves – and will not deliver the required outcomes.

The mandate comes from the CEO and the executive team. You need to make sure that the executive team is clear about the implications of the choices that they have made when creating the customer service strategy. Ask them to imagine how hard some of this will be, and get them to be prepared to face any difficult consequences. Bolster their resolve so that they will not surrender to the temptation to back away. Do this by asking them two questions: *'What is going to happen when this is being implemented?'* and *'Are you ready to confront the reality that there will be some impediments that you will have to overcome?'*

Ask them to list the impediments if you think they need to be clear. A little time invested at the beginning of a change programme can save a lot of uncomfortable back-flipping later.

A strong purpose

People need a good reason to make a change. Most frontline people do not want to suffer to make the shareholders richer, or the CEO's bonus larger. They need to have a reason that makes sense to them – from their point of view.

This means maintaining the same overall theme in your communications, but packaging it so that it relates to how people's jobs will be easier (free of frustrations, or more interesting, or more rewarding), how they will be able to serve customers better (so they spend less time getting yelled at), or how their opportunities to learn and develop will be improved (so they can advance).

When there is a strong personal reason for everyone to make the strategic projects work – then they will work.

A great exercise is to ask your senior managers to see the world through the eyes of the people at different levels in the business. Organise a one-hour meeting, and break them up into five groups. Allocate each group a different organisational level (front line, supervisors, middle managers, specialists, the top team) and ask each group to list what is important for the people at that level, and what needs to be included in the communication package so that it will appeal to those people.

Ask them to record their answers. It may be one of the most eye-opening exercises that your senior people have completed for a while.

Preparation

Have you ever painted a wall?

It is not the painting that takes the time. It is the cleaning, the filling, the application of the masking tape, and so on that is the most arduous part. It is tempting to skip all the preparation, ping the lid off the tin and roll on the paint. It will look great – for about six months.

In the seventh month the grease stains show through, you will start to be annoyed that the edges are so ragged and you will realise that the wall looks worse than it did before. Keep this image in mind because it neatly describes the need for preparing for a significant change.

The key elements that help to prepare your business for change are as shown in Figure 3.11.

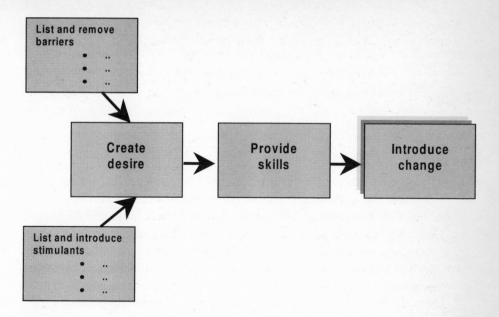

Figure 3.11   Preparing for change

People will change when they are good and ready to change. There are two ways to create this readiness. You need to both create desire and provide skills.

Create desire

The first part of creating desire is to identify the barriers that will make people resistant to change. List these barriers and specify what needs to be done to reduce the effect of those barriers.

The second is to identify what you need to do to introduce and stimulate an interest in the change that is coming. Create a list of the stimulants and then introduce those that will have the greatest impact. You need to be sure that the barriers and stimulants are being attended to before you start to introduce the skills required – otherwise the training provided will happen in a vacuum and will soon be forgotten.

Provide skills

Make sure that the new skills required are in place just in front of the next step – the actual implementation of the changes that you require. When you prepare the ground in this way, then the change will make sense and it will work.

The right people

You need to consider if you have the right people on two levels:

- the right people to be on the change team that will shepherd the change projects;
- the right people in the organisation to create a culture that will support your intended outcomes.

The right people on the change team

Even though your senior managers are the 'sponsors' of the customer service change projects, the chances are that everyone on your executive group is busy. They are probably working around 60 hours a week at the moment. That is already a crazy amount. The change projects are going to be juggled in with everything else – and will suffer.

You need to assemble a team of people who can be liberated from their normal duties so that they can do what it takes to advance the projects. They need to be smart, confident enough to speak up if they see a problem, and generally well respected. They are probably the most talented people in the middle layers of your organisation.

Ask the executive to create a list of these people, and gain the commitment that they will be given the time needed to implement the projects.

The culture that will support your intended outcomes

If you have people who are worn down by fear, who are worn out by long hours, and who are already working at the limits of their capability, then they will not be able to spontaneously 'break the rules to delight a customer'. Make sure that what is being asked of the people can be delivered (see Chapter 5).

Early wins

Any change process has its advocates and its enemies. The enemies are waiting for signs of trouble, looking for the chance to dismantle the change so that everything can go back to the way it was. You can probably think of a few people like that in your organisation.

Every change project needs to be able to prove that the decisions that have been made are correct, and the sooner the better.

It is worth identifying what can be progressed quickly and will definitely deliver what is promised. These are the early wins. A member of the change team should be given special responsibility for early wins.

Once these early wins are achieved they should be widely publicised.

Communication

Communication during the change process is typically handled poorly. The senior people put out tedious newsletters that are days behind the rumour mill. People complain that either they are told too little, or they are submerged in a blizzard of memos and e-mails. The secret is to find out what people want to know, tell them (preferably have their manager tell them in a group meeting so they have a chance to ask questions), and give them a chance to contribute their thoughts and ideas. If the previous steps have been completed properly then what needs to be communicated is pretty obvious.

So, a service strategy is developed at the intersection of your needs, customer expectations and process capabilities. It is progressed enthusiastically when it has strategic importance, it is animated by having a pound impact that is accepted by everyone, and it is articulated by the right people who have a personal stake in the successes of the outcome. The strategy is launched; now you need to keep it on track.

Using measures to stay on track

Imagine a stage. There are four actors in the foreground, each illuminated by a narrow-beam spotlight. In the gloom at the back of the stage are a further 50 performers. They are mere silhouettes.

Where do you focus your attention?

On those in the spotlight, right. The people in the background have to jump up and down and make a lot of noise before you are likely to see them at all.

Now, think about your measurement systems. Using the spotlight image, look at what parts of your organisation your measures put in the bright beam, and which parts are in the shadows.

Where is customer service?

The chances are that your organisation has plenty of measures that describe the way that money flows (because most measurement systems are designed by accountants). It is also highly likely that there will be few – if any – customer service measures used at a senior level, with the bulk of customer service data collected and used by the front line and their immediate supervisors/managers. The consequence is that customer service is at the back of the stage, unnoticed by people who are too busy talking about the financial situation.

This is perhaps the greatest contributor to organisational collapse in business today. Ask yourself, *'The leading organisations have the brightest people, the resources to fund initiatives, the customer contacts to develop new markets and the supply chains to create just about anything. . . so why is it that so many of these businesses fail?'* The answer is that they do not properly manage the drivers of tomorrow's opportunities, because they are too busy counting the effects of yesterday's success. Too often yesterday's success is not the same as tomorrow's opportunity.

The relationship you have with your customers is part of tomorrow's opportunity. Customer measures are an essential component in managing your capacity to gain the results that you need in the future.

There are two key activities:

- Develop a framework that emphasises the customer.
- Collect the right information.

Develop a framework that emphasises the customer

The gift of frameworks like the balanced scorecard is that they provide several headings that are important for organisational performance. One of these headings is 'customers'. Once this heading is inserted into board agendas, executive meetings, position descriptions, unit performance targets and bonus definitions, it becomes important.

If you do not have such a framework, then you need to develop one as soon as possible. If you need to convince the people at the top of your organisation that this is important, then show them the profit tree diagram (Figure 3.12).

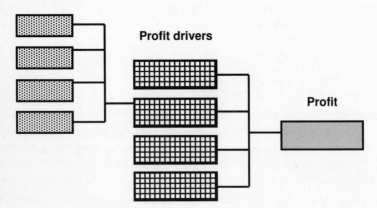

Figure 3.12 The profit tree

This is a powerful way to explain how an organisation really works (you wi
it again in the next chapter). Essentially, this model shows that profit – in the bo
on the right – is the consequence of properly managing a number of 'profit
drivers'. These profit drivers (typically there are four to six of them in most
organisations) are in turn made up from a set of key activities. It is at the activity
level that real control is exerted over a business.

So, if customer service is one of the key profit drivers in your business (which
is highly likely – since you are reading this book) then some of your profit is
delivered by activities that produce customer service. The better people are at
managing these activities, the more profitable the business will be.

Once people fully appreciate this concept, then talking about the money in the
business (the outcome) becomes a lot less important than talking about what
people can do to influence the activities that result in the money flowing (the
activities that make up customer service). When this happens, managers cannot
get away with trying to deliver profits simply by saying that they want it to go
up. Managers then do the real job that they are paid for: developing the context
and designing the processes that make it possible for work at the activity level
to be progressed smoothly (more on this in Chapter 4).

The department store was doing well. In fact, it had never done better. Costs were
down, and as a consequence profits were up. The new store manager was a hero.
The CEO gave him the most prestigious award at this year's 'dinner of champions'.

Now something was wrong. Profits had started to fall, gradually at first, and then
they tumbled. Loyal customers complained – and then defected. Employees were
resigning or requesting transfers in droves.

A team of consultants was called in – there must be a fundamental business driver
that was out of place. There was, except that it took no longer than 24 hours to find.
It became immediately apparent that it was the cost reduction programmes that drove
up profits. Casual hours were cut, employee numbers reduced, maintenance and
cleaning were downgraded – any opportunity to save a penny was taken.

The financial measurement systems all responded favourably, and these merely
served to reinforce the savagery of the store manager's cuts. The more he applied this
approach, the happier senior managers became and the greater the praise that he
received. The obvious problem (though not obvious to him) was that customer satisfaction was taking a real beating. In the beginning the customers who really liked the
store overlooked the scarcity of staff and the slightly scruffy appearance of the floors.

But they could only overlook it for so long before they complained. They could only
complain for so long before they went to the other department store down the road –
where they got the kind of service and experience that they wanted. Once they were
shopping somewhere else they did not come back – ever.

...w set of measures now. Right alongside the financial
...rs that show customer satisfaction, employee satisfaction
...iance. They are presented as an executive dashboard as
...3.

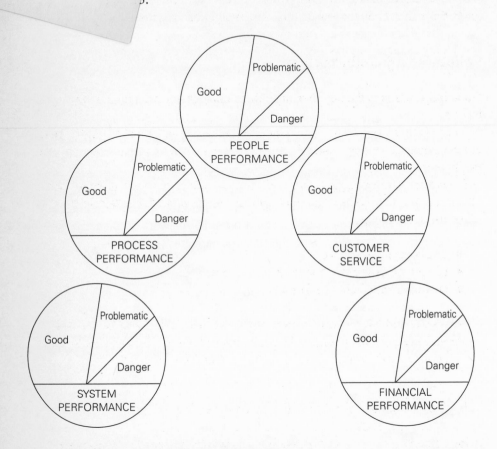

Figure 3.13   The executive dashboard

This is the front page of a report; on each subsequent page is another level of
detail that shows the position by store and then by departments and finally by
business unit.

The customer information comes from two sources – an analysis of performance against service standards, and an analysis of customer satisfaction (see
Chapter 9 for more on these).

When this business first introduced these measures they found that there were
several other stores that were close to making the same mistake as the new store

manager. The new information helped to avert a crisis. Once they were out of the danger zone the business worked on improving its customer and employee scores. The result was a slow but steady improvement in profits. This business will never again make the same mistake; they will now be able to make their gains through real improvements to fundamental business drivers.

Collect the right information

Good information is the key to being able to manage any activity in your organisation.

There are two key kinds of measurement data that you need to gather: performance against service standards, and customer satisfaction. These are covered in Chapter 9.

However, before you get there, spend a few minutes thinking about the kinds of information that you capture and keep at the moment. Consider these under three different headings:

- demographic data;
- service process performance information;
- customer satisfaction information.

Make a table and list the information that you collect today, and (as you reflect on the messages in this book) make some notes about the kind of data that you should collect in the future. The table should look like Table 3.5.

Table 3.5   Summary of information held and required

Information	Demographic data	Service process performance	Customer satisfaction
Information currently collected			
Information that should be collected in the future			

So, you are now in a position to develop the right kind of service strategy, get it implemented and maintain its importance through installing the right measures. You have made some fundamental decisions that will underpin future profitability and will deliver a specific customer experience. In the next chapters you will see how to get the most out of the money and resources that you will invest in those parts of your organisation that the customers touch directly.

4 *Extraordinary performance from 'ordinary' people*

The hotel was just as the brochure promised. Maybe even better.

The gold glistened, the marble was magnificent, the food was fantastic, the bedroom was beautiful, the pool was perfect and the gym was gigantic.

Sarah vowed that she would never return.

The service sucked.

There is a defining moment in customer service.

It is the moment when the customer talks to someone in your organisation. At this moment everything you represent is embodied in one person.

This humble individual is the ambassador for everyone you employ and everything you own. What they say and do tells the customer more about your organisation than any amount of advertising. On the basis of this interaction the customer may stay, come back with a friend, or go away – for ever.

Some organisations have got it right. The service you receive is neither smothering nor sulky, it meets your needs without forcing you to be like everyone else, and it makes you feel as if you are special. This experience does not happen by accident. It is the consequence of careful analysis, deliberate selection of key behaviours, and relentless monitoring and reinforcement.

You can deliver this kind of service as well, if you really focus on five key areas:

- selection;
- training;

- customer-centred management;
- culture development;
- frontline empowerment.

The first three of these are covered in this chapter; the next two belong to the next chapter.

Selection

Alan liked to see all his work in neat little piles. He liked to make a 'to do' list every day and be in control of his time. If it wasn't for the damned phone he would never have to take his fingers off the keyboard, or take his eyes off the screen.

Alan was the most productive and dedicated person in his section. He knew the systems. He knew the answer to just about any question. He was so good that he was given a big promotion. Alan became the key customer contact for enquiries.

By the end of the first week something was wrong. It wasn't that he suspected that he didn't like the job – he knew that he absolutely hated it. The customers asked their questions out of sequence, they did not understand what he said to them, and sometimes they were angry with him for no good reason.

Halfway through the second week Alan's boss got a complaint from a dissatisfied customer. By the end of the third week the number of complaints had risen to 20.

By the end of the fourth week Alan was found a new job. Not in his former department – his old job was already filled – but in a new part of the business, where Alan never performed at his original level again.

It happens over and over again. People are selected for customer contact positions because they have technical skills and/or expert knowledge. Too often they fail.

Most of the time those who fail stay in the position. They remain there for years, gradually poisoning the customers' perception of the organisation, and steadily undoing its capacity to be successful. In some organisations there are armies of the wrong kinds of people, who select others in their likeness because they know no better.

You need to approach selection with the clear understanding that not everyone is suited to a frontline position. Perhaps 1 in 10 people have what it takes to work behind a counter. Perhaps 1 in 10 of those can handle a call centre environment. The trick is to find the right ones.

One key difference between service organisations that deliver their chosen level of service at the most reasonable cost is that they are more thorough – and therefore spend longer – on the selection process. A lot longer. Where the average organisation whips through all the selection steps in 4 hours (or less) per person, the best organisations lavish up to 20 hours. There is a good reason for this investment.

Do the maths yourself. A really good person costs no more than a poor one. A good person will become productive more quickly, stay longer, be more able to accept additional levels of complexity, will take less management time, and will deliver more to your organisation every year than an average performer. When you 'buy' a person you are making a £150,000 purchase decision (an average of £15,000 for 10 years), which should be worth at least £450,000 in value (three times wages). That is a serious decision.

Choosing the right person is among the top five most critical decisions any organisation makes. Too often this decision is both poorly supported by facts and rushed through in a couple of weeks. The future of the business is frittered away by poor selection techniques placed in the hands of people who do not understand the cumulative impact of the choices that they have made.

There are four steps that you need to follow:

1. Understand the job.
2. Apply the right criteria.
3. Use the right tools.
4. Follow the right process.

Understand the job

People on the front line have high-level interpersonal challenges mixed in with mid-level technical problems, and high levels of repetition. This is a complex job. There is only one way to get a true appreciation of the kind of work that they perform. You need to go and have a look.

There are three steps that you need to complete before you are ready to define and describe a frontline position:

- observation;
- interviews;
- focus groups.

Observation

It is unlikely that anyone in a management position in your organisation will have a clear picture of what fills the day of a customer contact person. If you don't believe me, try asking a supervisor to describe the tasks and challenges faced by the front line, and then ask the people who do the work the same question. The chances are that there will be significant differences. Even those supervisors who used to perform frontline positions quickly lose touch.

If you spend two to four hours being very quiet and watching what people on the front line have to contend with every single day then you will gain a clear picture of the complexities of the work (see Chapter 2 for observation techniques).

The volumes were impressive. Every day thousands of documents flowed into the service centre. Every day they were all processed – even if it meant overtime. No wonder the work required 35 people. Or did it?

A little observation revealed that most documents were processed in considerably less than a minute. Even accounting for the time taken on the difficult cases, there was something wrong.

Patient observation over a couple of days uncovered the problem. It was the post. Not the arrival of the post, but the way in which it was sorted. Because the standard was to complete all processing each day, this meant that when people arrived in the morning they were dependent on the post for the next batch of work. The sorting job was the lowest-paid position in the group, and there was only one 'post sorter'. This sorter sifted through the whole post, and then categorised it and – when it was all done – she distributed it. This took about an hour.

It was an hour that the other 34 people spent reading the paper, chatting and generally filling in. This had been going on for years – and no one in management/ supervisory positions had noticed.

Interviews and focus groups

Once you are clear about what really happens, you can interview people individually and in groups. You should be testing your understanding, as well as gaining their perceptions about what are the most difficult parts of their work. You should also interview both the front line (to discover what really happens today) and the managers (to find out what should happen in the future).

Following your observation and the interviews/focus groups, you can then put together a clear description of the work, and the kind of person who is required.

Apply the right criteria

Take a look at the kinds of criteria on person specifications/position descriptions for customer contact jobs. Too many have the 'mock precision' of phrases like *'must be able to negotiate'* or *'must be a good communicator'*. These are descriptions that are empty of meaning, because words like 'communicate' have no standard definition. When you have woolly criteria, the wrong people will look like the right people. Those people end up in frontline positions where they feel miserable – and make your customers feel worse.

There are three key headings that you need to use to develop your criteria:

- knowledge/skills;
- personality characteristics;
- intelligence/IQ.

Knowledge/skills

It is entirely possible that there are myths surrounding the kinds of knowledge and skills your business really needs at the front line. These myths may be embodied in your selection criteria and expressed in your recruitment advertising.

Here is a straightforward exercise. Collect information that identifies your best frontline performers. You should look at sales achieved (if appropriate and/or available) as well as the experiences and outcomes achieved from the customer's point of view. Some simple observation and questioning should surface the information that you need.

If possible, get these people together in a room, but if not (because they are on different shifts/are in different locations), you will have to collect the information via the phone.

Ask them to provide the information required to complete Table 4.1 (ask them in person; their formal records may be out of date or inaccurate).

Table 4.1   Summary of key characteristics

Name	Education	Experience	Skills/abilities	Interests	One key differentiator

The kind of information that you should collect includes:

- **Education** – any kind of school/technical college/university qualifications.
- **Experience** – years of experience in different kinds of roles.
- **Skills/abilities** – all forms of special skills and abilities. You should look beyond work for skills like 'good at repairing my car' because these tell you something about the nature of the person.

- **Interests** – again, your questions should centre on work, but you should also collect data about strong interests in other parts of the person's life.
- **One key differentiator** – ask the person to consider themselves in relation to the other frontline people with whom they work. Ask them to state the biggest and most important difference between them and their workmates. This is a difficult question: the person may be modest, or they may not be able to articulate the difference easily. If this happens, ask them to describe a number of typical situations, and get them to describe what they do, and how it may differ from the way others respond.

Look for the themes and trends. Identify those characteristics that are common to all. Also, specify those characteristics that are held by the majority of the people you have spoken to. Now, create a template (using the same table) that truly reflects the knowledge and skills your front line requires.

This is only part of the picture. Aspects of knowledge/skills can be taught while personality and intelligence are considerably less flexible. Too many organisations use knowledge/skills as the key selection criteria (because they are easier to assess) in the hope that the other criteria will fall into place. This is a mistake. There is more that needs to be understood.

Personality characteristics

Finding the right kind of person is the key to delivering great service. Picking the right personality characteristics is the key to finding the right person.

A number of organisations have researched the personality profiles that deliver the right outcomes. One of the most respected and widely used profiles in the UK has been developed by Saville & Holdsworth Ltd (a UK-based international firm of psychologists). They have identified three groups of characteristics that are required for people in customer contact positions: relationships with people, thinking style, emotions. There are key personality elements for each of these, which are as follows.

Relationships with people

The key personality elements for relationships with people are as follows:

- persuasive – having the ability to negotiate and gain commitment (particularly in an area that handles complaints, or one where sales may be involved).;
- self-controlled – having the capacity to be restrained in showing irritation, and possessing patience;
- empathetic – having a sensitivity to others;

- modest – reluctant to talk about personal achievements;
- desiring to participate – having an inclination to be part of a team and develop constructive relationships;
- sociable – being talkative, and confident with different types of people.

Thinking style

The key personality elements for thinking style are as follows:

- analytical – enjoys, and is good at, working with facts and solving problems;
- innovative – develops a range of ideas and offers imaginative solutions;
- flexible – open to new approaches, and able to adapt to new situations;
- structured – plans ahead and is good at setting priorities;
- detail-conscious – is good with details, is neat and tidy;
- conscientious – makes sure that tasks are completed and fulfils commitments.

Emotions

The key personality elements for emotions are as follows:

- resilient – remains calm, copes with stress, and looks on the bright side;
- competitive – likes to win, and to be the best (particularly for positions that involve some sales);
- results oriented – sets ambitious personal targets, keen to improve performance;
- energetic – enjoys being active, sustains a high level of energy.

If your customer contact people possess a reasonable number of these characteristics, then you are going to be able to deliver noticeably good service. See worksheet 4 in the Appendix for a quick way to assess your people.

Intelligence/IQ

Intelligence is particularly difficult to define – even though we can all recognise someone who has it – and it is difficult to measure.

A great way to understand how the brain works is to think of it as a personal computer. The mix of games and programs is like the personality. The amount of data stored is like knowledge. The RAM and processor speed (in gigahertz) are like the two forms of intelligence.

There is the RAM-like intelligence, which is the capacity to keep many different concepts active at one time. This is the kind of intelligence that helps you to manage complexity. There is also the processor-like intelligence, which is the capacity to think quickly. This is about speed, and is often most evident in those who are highly articulate.

Some people have lots of RAM-like intelligence but little processor-like intelligence. They can see the big picture really clearly but need a lot of time to churn through these ideas, and may be borderline incoherent (think of the boffin scientist). Others have lots of processor-type intelligence, but little RAM. They may be amusing and crisp conversationalists, but have limited understanding about how the world really works. While their verbal skills will give them a head start, they quickly reach their limit in the organisational hierarchy (you know people like this).

Customer contact people need a reasonable amount of both kinds of intelligence. You can assess these during the selection process through the right kinds of written tests (there are many available), or through exercises (see later in this chapter).

Use the right tools

Most people are hired on the basis of their performance at an interview. They dress their best, present themselves in the best light, and are on their best behaviour. The chances are that you will not select the best applicant.

The interview is a good way to check facts and to gain an initial impression of the applicant, but most customer contact positions do not have a daily routine that looks like an interview. Performance at an interview is not the same as performance on the job. To test performance on the job, you need to be able to predict likely behaviour, and you need to simulate the kinds of challenges that the applicant will face every day.

Predicting behaviour is the function of the personality assessment against a scale – we have just covered this. Simulating real-life challenges is the function of exercises.

Exercises are remarkably easy to construct, and are painfully underused. There are seven steps that you need to follow:

1. Identify key activities that occur frequently. In your observations and interviews you will have discovered these.
2. Create a situation that simulates this activity. It may be a customer on the phone, an experience at a counter, and so on.
3. Write a scenario and a script so that either yourself or someone else can play the part of the customer reasonably consistently.

4. Write a list of the key points that you are examining, the process that you would like to see, and the outcome that should be achieved.
5. Write a background briefing you can give to the applicant so that they have an understanding of the required outcome, and they have enough facts to be able to resolve/progress the situation.
6. Now, ask the applicant to familiarise themselves with the background, and then challenge them to role-play their way through the situation.
7. Rate their performance against the list of key points, using a 1–5 scale, with 1 = flawless and 5 = poor.

Once you have conducted a couple of exercises you will be familiar with the roles, and you will have a powerful block of information to add to the selection decision.

Follow the right process

So, the selection process for customer contact people should include:

- an interview;
- a personality assessment and an IQ test;
- an exercise.

When you put these together they become an assessment centre – which is the method many best-practice organisations use for people in customer contact positions.

Applicants should be prepared to devote half a day to the process, and you will probably interview people in batches. You can then assess people using a strict set of criteria.

Is this a lot of effort? Yes it is. Is it worth it? Unequivocally.

Training

Take a look at your training expenditure for the past 12 months. It was probably in the order of 1–4 per cent of the amount you spent on payroll. That is a lot of money.

Now ask if you got value for money for that training. Consider two questions. *'Were your customer contact people able to better satisfy customers?'* and *'Did you introduce changes in behaviour that improved your bottom line?'*

These are hard questions to answer, because too much training is developed without a clear bottom-line statement of its effect, and without a way of measuring the financial benefit that has been achieved. This is a huge waste.

All training should be provided as a response to a specific need, in a way that produces a measurable – bottom line – outcome. (If you are interested in this, then have a look at an article on measuring HR projects and processes on Neville Lake's Web site: www.lakegroup.com.au.) This is particularly important when designing training for frontline positions. In the customer contact world, there are specific experiences that you want to create, and particular outcomes that you want to achieve. Training should achieve these outcomes, and the effect of this training should be ruthlessly assessed.

As far as customer service training is concerned, there are two key challenges: bringing everyone to the minimum standards required, and creating flexibility.

Bringing everyone to the minimum standards required

Kelly was so pleased to get the job. She was the first person from her school to be offered a full-time position. Now it was her first day, and she had spent hours getting ready. Everything she was wearing was new, and she felt as though she had stepped straight out of a catalogue.

'Thank heavens you are early,' her new boss had wailed. 'Jenny is sick so you will have to go straight onto reception. You will pick it up really quickly.'

That was it. That was Kelly's briefing. Her boss was gone as rapidly as she had appeared, spirited away in a cloud of stress. The phone started to ring. People started to arrive. Kelly took off her new coat, but didn't even know where to hang it.

Often it is your most junior people who are responsible for the day-to-day relationship with your customers. How often have you been 'assisted' by a temp struggling away in a key role – the sum of their knowledge dependent on a full five-minute briefing?

Everyone needs to be able to perform at a minimum standard, and this means that you need to pay particular attention to two areas: 'induction' and 'training to achieve standards'.

Induction
Everyone knows how hard it is not only to settle into an established workgroup but also to learn all the quirky little details that make up a new job. Everyone knows this, and yet for many new starters induction is still an unstructured,

muddled set of hasty introductions and broken instructions from the person who sits next to them.

If you want to give the customer a consistent experience, then there is no way around developing a solid induction package. This should contain three elements:

- context information – so that the person can position your organisation in the marketplace;
- corporate information – which explains how your organisation is put together, and how the work group the person has just joined fits into the total structure;
- content information – which covers the details of the job, provides a way to assess where skill gaps may exist, delivers a training solution to bridge those gaps, connects the new starter with a person who can help them when needed, and specifies when they will be ready to work without assistance/supervision.

Training to achieve standards

Many service interactions are repetitive. While the circumstances and outcome may be different, the process is much the same. This means that the skills and knowledge that deliver the required behaviours can be taught. The best way to do this is as follows:

1. List the types of work that are completed. You will probably find that there are clusters around different 'stations' (such as inbound calls, counter services, reception, and so on).
2. Find out what behaviours and outcomes the customers expect (see Chapters 1 and 2).
3. Deduce the behaviours that will deliver the customer experience your organisation wants to provide (see Chapter 3).
4. Design a way to observe the required behaviours.
5. Develop a list of the skills and knowledge that underpin those behaviours.
6. Assess everyone to be sure that they evidence those behaviours. There should be a card for each that specifies the behaviours observed (at least three times) by trained supervisors, and which has a space for signed confirmation that the individual is proficient in that activity.
7. If the right behaviour is absent, then the missing knowledge/skill should be identified and training should be provided.
8. If someone who is deemed to be proficient is observed to lapse, then remedial training can be provided.

This is a more focused application of training than most organisations are used to, and the assessment component means that the emphasis is on the behaviour change – not the completion of the training activity. Some organisations award stars or badges to those who have been assessed – and passed. These are among the organisations that are seen to deliver the best service in the world.

The hotel chain knew what their customers wanted. They knew because they had asked them – and asked them often.

The customers wanted to be treated as 'guests': they wanted to feel as if they had come to a place that was familiar and where people knew them – particularly if they were a regular guest, but even if this was the first time they had visited that particular location, they wanted a level of personalised service that they could not find anywhere else. Delivering against this level of expectation needs a special approach.

For this hotel chain it begins with selection. There is a remarkably well-defined and strictly adhered to set of criteria. One of these is 'relationship extension', which means that people are good at remembering names, lots of them (this is tested). Only those people who have an encyclopedic capacity to remember names and attribute them to the right person get the job.

Next come the processes. The people who take the baggage out of the car have to get the suitcases to the front desk before the guest arrives. This way the people on reception can read the bag tags and identify the guest. They can call up the guest information on their computer. The system contains all kinds of guest preferences. In fact, every time a guest asks for something it is recorded. This means the receptionist can say something like 'Welcome again to this hotel. I hope you enjoyed your time in New York. We have given you a room with a view of the park at the top of the building, and we have put your special brand of water in the fridge.' The registration card is printed with all the necessary information; all that is needed is a signature.

Then comes the training. Each piece of behaviour that makes up the greeting, sharing of information, processing on the computer and handling any questions is defined and described. The receptionists are fully trained in each one, covering not only what they have to do, but also why achieving that outcome is important. They work through a number of levels of skills, and when their supervisor thinks that they are ready they are assessed. This assessment means that they have to know what to do, and then their behaviour is observed. If they perform the behaviours correctly a number of times they get a certificate.

That is how guests get to feel as though they have 'come home' every single time they check in.

Creating flexibility

People come and go, the kinds of tasks that need to be completed change with the level of demand, and new products/services are developed. Customer contact people need to be able to move across a number of different skill groups to ensure that service standards are maintained – whatever the circumstances. This means deliberately providing additional skills and knowledge to a reasonable percentage of the people.

If you design your training in the way just described then it is relatively easy to develop a portfolio of assessed skills for each frontline person. An effective 'low-tech' way to do this is to have all the people on the front line who have mastered the skills/knowledge required for their current position actively learning new skills. When they have been assessed as being proficient at the new skills/knowledge then they are awarded a certificate. In this way, each person gradually increases the number of certificates they hold. The number and spread of certificates in your organisation is a measure of your flexibility.

Customer-centred management

You can spend as much time and money as you have to select and develop frontline employees, but all this will be wasted if they are not managed in a way that enables them to deliver their best outcomes. To get the right kind of service for your business, your managers need to be customer centred.

To be customer centred they need to have the right model of what being a manager is really all about. In the book *The Third Principle* Neville Lake introduced two key models that apply to all management situations, but are particularly relevant to managing in a customer service business. These are 'the pretend manager' and the 'pathfinder manager'.

The pretend manager

The coach doors hissed open. 'Eiffel Tower', shouted the tour guide, 'Fifteen-minute photo stop.'

Sally tumbled out of the door. The morning light stabbed at her hangover. She handed David her camera, and stood by the short wall. She glanced over her shoulder to make sure that the distant tower would be in the picture. She forced a smile as David dutifully fired off three shots.

'Do you want me to take one of you?', she asked.

'Nah,' he replied, 'you can take me next time, I'll get a copy of yours.' He looked around. 'Where is this?'

'Paris.'

'I'll do Rome', he said, heading back to the bus.

On the 17-day bus tour of Europe people get the chance to 'do' Paris, Rome, Athens, and so on. They boast to their friends that they have visited all those places. However, squinting into the camera with the Eiffel Tower in the background and gaining a real appreciation of the Parisian way of life are completely different – even if the photographic evidence is the same.

Many management activities are completed in the same way. Too many 'managers' perform the peripheral functions, and yet they do not make the contribution that is available to them. Too many managers have meetings where nothing of value happens, they run improvement projects that produce little change, and they collect and report information that will not be used. They have 'done' the job of managing, and they have involved other managers – who in turn will involve them – in all kinds of activities that replace real work. This is all so subtle that people do not see what is really going on.

Cross-selling was a problem. It was the biggest problem that the sales manager had to solve. He wrote reports that showed what level of cross-selling was possible and what was actually achieved, he talked about it in meetings, he spent money on training. He had done what he could. Yet the level of cross-selling had hardly changed.

The CEO was so concerned that she started to ask questions – detailed questions about activities and outcomes.

The sales manager produced a file that proved that all the frontline people had been to the training, and there was the attendance register to prove it. However, there was no analysis of the dimensions of the problem, no study to show what could be achieved, no assessment of who needed to know what, no analysis of the behaviours that needed to change, and no evaluation of whether or not any change occurred. It looked good on paper – but on paper is not where the changes need to occur.

The core of the problem is that it can be easy to confuse the activity with the outcome, and to mistake surface effort for real achievement. This is pretend managing. It can be tiring, it does take up a lot of time, and it is more often than not devoid of personal satisfaction. It is pretend managing that is to blame for the failure of many excellent programmes.

'Oh, we did TQM,' people will tell you, 'but it didn't work.' What they do not say – what they may not even know – is that the programme should have been more than a series of expensive training courses, more than a few obvious projects, and deserved a lot more senior management attention than it received.

'I have made it clear that performance needs to improve,' a divisional head might say, having just told his immediate reports to 'Get your profits up – or you will be looking for another job.' What this manager will not tell you is that while this exhortation felt good, without any guidance on what was possible and where the opportunities were hiding, none of the subordinates was any better off – they were just more anxious.

'I spend all my time in meetings,' an overworked manager will explain to a customer who has been waiting for an answer for several days. This manager will probably not be able to tell that maybe a third should not have been held at all (they were really a single person's responsibility and group decision-making was simply a way to dilute accountability), maybe another third could have been better served by someone else, and those that remained could have been half as long.

Pretend managing destroys frontline performance, and it costs your business money and opportunities – a lot of money and opportunities. The way to expose pretend managing is to focus on achievement. This means making sure that managers keep a diary that shows how they have made a contribution to the business every single day. It means that every manager needs to be able to isolate the effects of their effort and show what they have done to increase profit. It means that individuals need to take accountability for outcomes.

This is a painful level of analysis for some managers, but it is an essential activity. While pretend managing is a problem for any business, it really gets in the way in service organisations because the service interactions are delivered by the front line, and they can only produce the right outcomes if they are put in a position where they can be successful. If the managers are not doing their job, then life at the front line will always be a struggle and the customer experience will forever be less than happy.

To be able to put the front line 'on a playing field where they can win', managers need to be pathfinders.

The pathfinder manager

There are lots of words to describe managers. The manager as a 'coach', as a 'cheerleader', as an 'inspiration' (you wish), and so on. These images do not do justice to the power that a manager has to shape the destiny of the business. A new image is needed. It is the image of the manager as a pathfinder. This implies analysis coupled with action, it suggests decision making and it is about having a purpose. It is a particularly useful image for those in the service business.

There are four key aspects of the pathfinder's role:

- reconnaissance;
- design;

- barrier clearing;
- enabling people to act.

Reconnaissance

Danni was told to ask questions. To ask anything she liked. After all, how can you learn if you don't ask?

'So, how many people come into the store every day?' She thought she would start with something easy, but the store manager did not know.

'Of those who come in, what percentage buy something?' The store manager did not know.

'What percentage that do buy something also buy an accessory that is intended to go with the item?' The store manager did not know that either.

'How many people look around in here, and then go to our competitors across the street and buy the item there?'

The store manager was starting to get angry. 'Don't you have any proper questions for me?', he asked.

Danni thought for a while. 'What can you tell me about the fundamental drivers that make this store successful?'

The store manager relaxed. 'I can tell you about cash taken, about sales per square foot, about casual hours and overtime and about stock turnover.'

'And what do those indicators tell you about the business?', she asked, already guessing the answer.

'We are not doing as well as we hoped.'

In every organisation there are all kinds of variables that bob around like corks on a sea – and there is nothing that you can do about them. There are, however, a number of key drivers in any business that are (at least to some degree) able to be controlled. It is the job of the pathfinder manager to identify these drivers.

This is an amazingly difficult task. It is not uncommon to find that the measures people believe are the key drivers are really a list of those items that are easy to count and record (and sometimes these are even symptoms of the effects of variables that they cannot control). It is not unusual to discover that the way in which processes have been designed, the way they are operated by the front line, and the way the supervisors think they work are three different stories altogether. Too often the true value the customer really wants is not understood, and so effort is wasted on providing unappealing features while some real benefits are undelivered.

The reason that these kinds of problems persist is that businesses are remarkably complex – much more complex than most people realise. Consider a game of chess. How many moves do you think are possible during a single game? Thousands, tens of thousands, hundreds of thousands, millions perhaps? The answer is a surprising 10^{108}. That is 10 with 108 noughts after it. That is a big number.

Now, think how much more complex your business is than a single game of chess. Indeed, think about how much more complex a frontline position is than a single game of chess. To cut through that complexity the pathfinder manager has to spend a lot of time analysing the business, and what really – fundamentally – underpins success and drives failure. This means that the pathfinder manager needs to use a lot of analysis tools with both customers and employees, such as:

- process mapping;
- histograms;
- analysis of variation;
- sub-optimisation analysis;
- socio-technical systems analysis;
- observation;
- focus groups;
- surveys;
- benchmarking;
- and so on.

This means that the manager needs to spend a lot of time thinking and researching. Not every manager is comfortable doing this. In this era of 'knowledge work', many businesses still want their managers to be applying the 'muscle work' principles of always doing and closely supervising. This is not a winning formula in this millennium.

Once the pathfinder manager has discovered what is really making the business tick, then he or she needs to create the best ways for outcomes to be produced.

Design

There is no end-point. There is no moment where perfection has been achieved. Every business is changing, developing, and having to respond to new challenges and opportunities.

There is a constant need to design and redesign the way in which outcomes are achieved, and this is clearly the role of the pathfinder manager. No one else can do it in the business. The front line are busy on the day-to-day activities, senior managers have strategic issues to worry about. This is where managers truly have a chance to make a difference.

Think about all those businesses that have gone through a major process redesign in the past few years. Have you ever wondered what all the managers were doing in those businesses that the processes became so fat, sloppy and cumbersome that a major intervention was needed just to bring them into line with the rest of the industry? It is entirely possible that the managers were trapped being pretend managers and frittering away their time in meetings that made minimal difference at the end of the day anyway.

Design involves using all the information gathered and finding the best way for the processes, systems and people to function so that the customers get the best possible outcome for the costs the business needs to incur in accordance with the strategic plan. The trick is to use an 'iterative model', which means developing something to a certain level and then trying it in a limited way, learning from the experience, trying it again, and so on. This means that the new design has most of the bugs hammered out of it before it is applied across the whole business.

It is entirely possible that a pathfinder manager will spend 50 per cent or more of his or her time on reconnaissance and design.

Barrier clearing

Australia is a harsh country. The sun slices through the thin layers of ozone to scorch life into the vegetation. Sometimes the rain does not fall for months at a time.

The soft, papery leaves that adorn the coddled European trees would be seared off their branches. The Australian leaf is like a blade of plastic. It cannot wilt. It stays rigid long after it has fallen off the tree.

Consequently, the leaf litter is an impenetrable mat. Nothing in the soil can break through. No seeds can force their roots down.

The very feature that keeps the trees alive – their indestructible leaves – will rob them of their future.

The solution is fire. The Australian bush needs a fire to burn away the leaves and expose the soil. For this reason, many of the native plants have seed pods that will open only when exposed to temperatures over 100°C.

The sad truth is that businesses are bristling with barriers. They need their own form of life-giving fire to clear away the past and be healthy for the future. It is the pathfinder manager who needs to apply the blowtorch.

The good news is that the barriers are easy to find. Two straightforward techniques are barriers boards and focus groups.

Barriers boards

People know where the barriers are in their work area. Because these problems are so obvious to them, they probably think that you know too, but for some reason you have not acted yet.

You need to explain the concept of complexity (maybe use the chess game as an illustration) and make it clear that it is highly likely – or just about inevitable – that there will be barriers in their work area. Set up a number of barriers boards that people can use to list the barriers that get in their way at work, with their suggestions about a solution and their observations about the likely impact.

Table 4.2   The barriers board

Barrier that gets in your way	What effect does this barrier have on the business?	What is a possible solution?	Any other comments

Typically these boards are stuck on noticeboards, but you could also provide forms or e-mail opportunities. You will be amazed at how many ideas you will get within a week of making these available.

Focus groups

The process of designing and running focus groups has been covered already (see Chapter 2). This is another topic that is worth exploring using this technique. You should make sure that you cover all parts of the business, from the front line through to the senior managers, and both the operational and support areas of the business.

Using these techniques you will discover an alarming quantity of barriers – too many to fix in the short term. Therefore you need to prioritise this list to make it more manageable. To do this you need to create a set of criteria that you can use to sort the barriers. These criteria will probably include items such as:

- Cost impact – the costs that this barrier is producing (ie the costs that would be removed if the barrier was destroyed) for the whole business. Use a score of 1–10, with 10 as high (if the cost is high, then give it 10).
- Sales impact – the total value of the sales that are being lost. Use a score of 1–10, with 10 as high.

- Cost to fix – the total cost to fix this barrier, including time invested, resources and system changes. Use a score of 1–10, but now 1 is high (if the cost is large, then score 1).
- Time required to fix – the number of weeks it will take before the barrier can be removed. Use a score of 1–10, with 1 as high (if it takes a long time, then score 1).
- Strategic importance – the importance of removing this barrier to the strategic direction of the business. Use a score of 1–10, with 10 as high.

You can then place your barriers in a table as shown in Table 4.3.

Table 4.3 Analysis of barriers

Barrier	Cost impact	Sales impact	Cost to fix	Time required	Strategic importance	Total score

Add up the scores and place them in the total score column. Use this column to re-sort the list into a rank order. This will be about 85–95 per cent accurate. Apply a little common sense to this list, and produce a rank order. Draw a line under the top 20 per cent. These are the barriers that deserve your urgent attention.

Once you have stripped out as many of the barriers as possible, you need to start the process again. Barriers will always return. A well-designed process will change by at least 20 per cent every two years as a response to frontline and supervisory interventions. Not all of that change will be good.

Enabling people to act
There are three aspects of enabling people to act:

- being hard on non-performers;
- applying the six ingredients of management;
- boosting performance.

Being hard on non-performers
How many non-performers are there in your organisation? One in 100? One in 50? Maybe more?

There is every chance that more than 1 in 50 people is consistently perform-ing below the acceptable standards your business requires. These people have effectively resigned – it is just that they keep on coming to work. It is equally likely that this non-performance is spread throughout the organisation. Take a look at your non-performing managers; they are jeopardising not only their own job, but all the jobs that report to them.

Every day that this non-performance is allowed to continue, you are sending the message *'We don't really care.'* You are effectively saying, *'We know that your manager is not doing her job, but we don't want to have an unpleasant conversation with her'* or *'We know that James on the front line is not giving customers the best outcome, but we are not going to do anything about it.'* When you let those messages persist, they will sap your efforts to deliver service.

The simple (and uncomfortable) truth is that poor performance is never a secret. If you were to survey a group of employees and ask them to nominate the poor performers – then everyone would provide you with the same list of names. The unavoidable (and even more uncomfortable) truth is that most people will – at some time in their lives – be a poor performer. If no one says anything, and no one offers any kind of assistance, then you can get stuck in that state for far too long – maybe for ever.

The pathfinder manager is paid to do a job. Part of that job is to set standards and to monitor performance to make sure that those standards are met by every-one. If someone starts to 'go off the boil' then the pathfinder is obliged to say something. It is not personal – it is simply what everyone expects him or her to do. After all, no one likes to carry an under-performing colleague, or to suffer under an uninterested boss.

The steps that need to be followed to identify poor performance, bring it to someone's attention, identify causes, create a remedial plan and put this into effect are already well known to managers. The real problem is getting every manager to do this as part of their job.

Applying the six ingredients of management

The six ingredients of management have been mentioned in one way or another in this chapter and will be in the next. However, it is worth bringing them all together so that they can be seen as a complete set. The six ingredients are:

- Take responsibility for outcomes.
- Set realistic goals.
- Provide the right steering mechanisms.
- Get information to the right places at the right time.

- Provide the tools to get the work done.
- Develop the right skills.

Take responsibility for outcomes

Being busy does not count. Attending meetings is not an end in itself. Being at the central point of all workflow is definitely not it. While these may seem like legitimate ways to describe and measure management time, there is only one true way to assess a manager, and that is by what they produce.

This is a particularly challenging notion for some managers – particularly those who are primarily responsible for customer service. It means that managers have to establish ways to measure the outcomes produced by the group of people for whom they are responsible, and also isolate the contribution that they have made.

It is also particularly important for managers involved in service, because customers are not interested in how busy you are, or how many meetings you have attended, or how challenging the problems are. They just want results. Therefore your measurement processes should talk about the way in which you have delivered those results.

Set realistic goals

The graph told the story. The 'target' line shot up optimistically, showing that every month should be an improvement on the month before. The 'actual' line had a considerably less impressive incline. The difference was shaded in red. There was a lot of red.

Every morning people looked at the chart. No one knew how the targets had been set, no one knew what to do, no one felt motivated to try any harder.

You may have seen this kind of graph. You may have been given these kinds of targets. They may have been called 'stretch targets', but the only thing that was really stretched was your belief that those managers who set the targets really knew what they were doing.

Those goals that underestimate the capacity of the people/processes/system will develop boredom. Those goals that are beyond the reaches of the team will be debilitating. The right goals will be met.

It is the pathfinder manager's job to analyse the business and the market, and to calculate the level of performance that is possible. It is his or her job to explain how goals can be met and it is up to the pathfinder to be realistic about giving individuals and the team a level of decision making that is within their capability, and a level of complexity that is within their understanding.

Provide the right steering mechanisms

A ship at sea gets pulled around by the currents and blown around by the wind. There is the constant need to make corrections to keep the vessel on course. It is the same with business. The pathfinder manager needs to have the following:

- a clearly defined 'destination': knowing what outcomes need to be produced, what activities and behaviours lead to those outcomes and what levels of performance are required;
- a sensitive way to measure progress: this includes measures for all of the above;
- a feedback loop, so that the information about progress can be matched with the ambition about the destination – and corrections can be made.

Consider your business, particularly the processes completed by the front line. Do you have the steering mechanisms that you need (see Chapters 3 and 9)?

Get the right information to the right place at the right time

The pathfinder manager needs to be clear about who needs what kind of information by when. You need to ask this question with a completely open mind. It is highly likely that the formal information systems that you have today do not provide all the information that people on the front line really need. It may even turn out that those on the front line do not have a clear idea about what they need; they are so used to asking someone for an answer that they do not recognise that there is an information gap.

You will probably have to use a mixture of careful observation and interviews, and maybe also do a frontline job yourself and see where you run out of the data you need.

Provide the tools to get the work done

People at the front line need computer systems that work, structures that do not fall down, machines that can make the products and ways to deliver services. They look to the pathfinder managers for all they need to be successful.

Develop the right skills

The training section in this chapter covered the formal acquisition of skills. There are many more subtle skills that need to be learnt. These kinds of skills include:

- the way to stop meetings from running too long;
- the way to handle different types of customers;
- the way to work in a team where not everyone likes you.

These are the kinds of skills that support good performance at work. These are the kinds of skills that can be coached by the pathfinder manager.

Boosting performance

Ordinary people are capable of extraordinary performance. Just look at what happens when there is some kind of emergency or crisis. To achieve this level of performance (at least some of the time) and to get somewhere close (the majority of the time), you need the following:

- clarity of task and outcome;
- rewards and celebration;
- a sense of purpose.

Clarity of task and outcome

The builder made careful notes. He wanted to be clear about what the owner wanted. He asked a lot of questions, knowing that he would need to prepare a detailed quote.

His quote was not the cheapest, but it was the most thorough, and represented value for money. Every day the owner met with the builder while the work was being done. They reviewed progress, discussed any problems and the owner always made sure that she was getting exactly what she wanted. There was never any doubt about what had to be done, by when and what it should look like.

When you employ a builder you know the end result you want, and you check often to make sure that you get this outcome. When you employ a team of people at work it gets a lot more confusing. It is unbelievably difficult to deliver 'extraordinary performance' when you are not exactly sure what you need to do, and your map to help you get the right outcomes is poorly drawn. It is for the pathfinder to provide clarity of task and outcome.

Rewards and celebration

We have already covered the need for rewards. It is for the pathfinder manager to recognise the reasons to reward and to create the circumstances that enable celebration. Small successes can be highlighted if they make a big point, daily triumphs can be celebrated if it stimulates more of the same, and dramatic outcomes can be matched with equally spectacular hoopla.

A sense of purpose

The experimenters gave each participant a booklet of detailed mathematical calculations. There would be no calculators, no talking and a tight time limit.

After the allocated period a bell sounded and all the booklets were collected. The
chief examiner unceremoniously tore them up and threw them in the bin. Everyone was
stunned.

New booklets of equally challenging problems were distributed, and once again
people worked away in silence to produce as many correct answers as possible. The
same thing happened again: all the booklets were torn up and dumped in the bin.

A third set of booklets appeared, to be greeted by a small mutiny. People complained, they shook their fists at the examiner and they walked out. Those who remained
dutifully completed the booklets, only to watch them being torn up and added to the
pile of paper on the floor.

This process went on for hours, until the final person had enough, and the examiner
was left alone in the room.

While people will continue to complete tasks that have little meaning to the
customers or themselves for a considerable period of time (particularly if they
are being paid), there comes a point where enough is enough, and they leave. On
the journey to that point they will become increasingly sloppy, they will invest
less and less of themselves and they will take advantage of every intended (and
unintended) perk your business can provide.

You never want to get people started down this slippery slope. The pathfinder
manager in a customer service-oriented business needs to anchor what people are
doing firmly in the reality of the effect they are having on their customers.
Customer research and feedback breathes life into daily activities, and achievement can be measured by the effect that is achieved.

So, take the right people, give them the right skills, give them a manager who
understands how to create the mechanism and context that produces good service
– and you have the recipe for a great customer experience – as long as the culture
is right. For this see the next chapter.

5   *Creating the culture that compels great service*

There is no doubt that culture makes a difference. For service-oriented organisations, it can make *the* difference. A good culture focuses people on what they can do to achieve both happy customers and sound financial performance. It is a powerful asset. It can be worth up to 30 per cent more on your bottom line.

In a landmark study – described in their book *Corporate Culture and Performance* – John Kotter and James Heskitt found that:

> Firms with cultures that emphasised all constituencies (customers, stockholders and employees) and leadership from all managers outperformed firms that do not have those cultural traits by a huge margin. Over an 11-year period the former increased revenues by an average of 682 per cent versus 166 per cent for the latter, expanded their workforces by 282 per cent versus 36 per cent, grew their stock price by 901 per cent versus 74 per cent and improved their net incomes by 756 per cent versus 1 per cent.

That is pretty persuasive. However, mention culture to a group of seasoned managers and many will groan. They may be polite and keep it inside, but the groan will be there anyway.

There are few managers who have not been burnt by the huge investment of money, time and ego in a 'culture renewal' programme. These managers have suffered endless training programmes, and they still have a drawer full of coffee cups, mouse mats and desk ornaments that reinforce the now forgotten slogans.

Many of these culture change programmes either failed outright, or fizzled out after a couple of years. The search for the right culture was always a worthy pursuit. It is simply that these programmes looked in the wrong place. The trick to designing and sustaining a service culture is to understand that the right kinds of people know how to deliver good service.

If you do not have the right people, then go back a few pages to the section on selection in Chapter 2. If you do have the right people (or at least enough of them) but they do not behave in the right way, then the reason is almost certainly that either service is made unimportant or they are prevented from giving the customer a good experience – or both.

Behaviour in organisations is the consequence of a number of important drivers that collectively tell people what is important and that regulate their options. This is one of the most important sentences in this chapter, so let me say it again: 'Behaviour in organisations is the consequence of a number of important drivers that collectively tell people what is important and that regulate their options.' Once you understand this, then getting results through people is a whole lot easier. This chapter shows you how to understand and control the key drivers of culture, both in general terms and with specific reference to frontline empowerment.

The drivers of culture

These drivers are a mixture of the obvious and the subtle, but every day they scream at your people to behave in a particular way – the way they are behaving today. Change the messages, and you will change your culture. These drivers are:

- management attention;
- management example;
- feedback from your immediate manager/supervisor;
- reward systems;
- the way that the structure confers status.

Management attention

Try this simple experiment. Find a tall building (preferably one that your organisation owns) in a capital city. Stand at street level and concentrate on the experience. Be aware of the buzz of the traffic, the blur of people rushing by, the smell of machinery and buildings, the effect of the weather conditions.

Now, travel in the lift to the executive floor at the top of the building, and look out of the CEO's window.

You could be on another planet. Your surroundings are quiet, unhurried, and sanitised by air conditioning. You can see the gleaming cliffs of windows, the clean edges of the surrounding office blocks, the hills in the distance and the sky above. The individual people and the traffic are tiny and insignificant.

The CEO's view of the business is much the same. Aggregated figures represent activities, numbers of employees replace individual names, trend information about customer preferences takes the place of gut instinct built on daily contact, and relentless waves of financial data feed mathematical models that are supposed to show whether the organisation is still on track.

The most common mistake senior managers make is to think that their view of the organisation will make sense to those on the ground floor, and these managers talk to the front line as if they all made the long journey in the lift every morning. Making a profit may be the all-consuming goal for those at the top, it may even be interesting to everyone, but profit is not an outcome that the front line can achieve.

The profit tree (Figure 5.1) is a powerful way to help those at the top to understand how to get the messages right, and through these, how to talk to the front line so that they behave in a way that ultimately delivers the right outcomes.

It is a powerful way to explain how an organisation really works (you have seen it already in Chapter 3). Essentially, this model shows that profit – in the

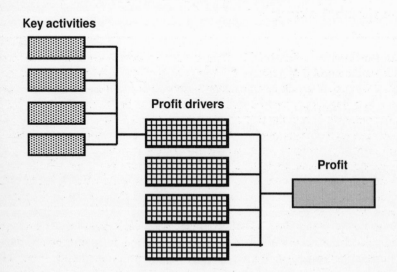

Figure 5.1 The profit tree

box on the right – is a blunt measure. Profit is the consequence of properly managing a number of 'profit drivers'. These profit drivers (typically 4–6 of them in most organisations) are in turn made up from a set of key activities (maybe 20–40 in total). It is at the activity level that real control is exerted. Make a list of what these are in your business.

You can now see the 20–40 key activities that deliver profits to your organisation. These are activities that you can control. This is where you should have the key measures for your organisation, and it is these activities that senior managers should talk about with frontline employees.

Two outcomes immediately flow when senior managers start to talk about the activities at this level. The first is that they connect with customer contact people. Now the people at the top are talking about activities that they recognise (not the more general concept of profit, which they do not). Second, by specifying what they want to happen at the activity level, those at the front line know what they have to do, and can respond in a way that delivers the intended outcome.

You will find that instead of talking about money, senior people are talking about customers. Instead of lamenting about being below budget, they are telling stories about service, and instead of exhorting people to do better, they are providing concrete examples of what they want. When senior people talk about customers a lot, then customers become important, and you can build a customer service culture.

Management example

'Customer service,' said the CEO, 'that is our number one priority.' He beamed out at the assembled group of managers. 'From now on we will go out of our way to delight every customer. We will create customer stories that will be passed from person to person in coffee shops, over family dinners and at the board table. We will be the envy of our competitors, and the best retailer our customers have visited.'

That was six months ago. Since then the CEO had given that speech dozens of times, up and down the country – but nothing had really changed.

'I just don't understand it,' he sighed. All the senior people were baffled.

A consultant was called in. 'Tell me what you do,' he said. The CEO started to reiterate what he had said. 'No,' said the consultant, 'tell me what you do. For example, what do you do when you visit a store?'

'I always make sure that everything is in order. I check on the stock, the fixtures and fittings, the condition of the public areas and those out of sight. Then I go through the financials with the store manager. We look at takings, casual hours, sales per square foot and so on.' The CEO paused. 'Oh. Wait a minute, I think I may have made a mistake.'

'What kind of mistake?' prompted the consultant, knowing that the penny had dropped.

'Well, if people looked at where I put my attention they might think that what is really important is the stock, fixtures and fittings and so on – and not the customers at all.' He went quiet for a while. 'I think I will try something different next time.'

The next day the CEO visited a key store in a major city. He served some customers himself (much to everyone's surprise, and with a small amount of embarrassment when he could not operate the cash register). He asked employees to tell him stories about how they had done more than expected for customers. He took those stories to the next store, and listened to theirs. Soon the word went around that customers really were important, and the programme started to work.

Feedback from your immediate manager/supervisor

While senior managers set the tone, it is your immediate boss that has the greatest impact on what you value and where you spend your time. From childhood onwards, we are very good at working out what we have to do to please the people around us. We all apply this mixture of instincts and fine-tuned learning to our managers.

Essentially, no one listens to what their boss says is important. We all watch his or her behaviour. If the boss in interested in certain activities or outcomes, then we will gravitate to those first. If the boss spends his or her time on certain kinds of work, we take an interest in that kind of work. If the boss sees customers as unwelcome interruptions that spoil his or her day – then there is no way that we will be able to be fully customer oriented.

All of this is subtle. It can be difficult to work out the kinds of behaviours and activities that are being reinforced. You need to:

- identify the behaviours that your business needs to evidence;
- identify the extent to which they are present;
- introduce changes if required.

Identify the behaviours that you need

There are six steps you need to follow to develop a list of the behaviours that your organisation needs to evidence. These are:

1. Organise four groups of experienced customer contact staff who have been in your organisation for no less than three years. Four people in each group, for about an hour.

2. Ask each group a specific question: *'What is it that managers (you have worked for) in this business need to do to help you to deliver service to your customers?'* Ask them to get a clear picture in their mind of the best manager, and the worst.
3. Ask each person to list (on a piece of paper) the key differences between the best and the worst, concentrating on what it was that the best people do.

Table 5.1 Revealing key management/supervisory behaviours

	Best person	**Worst person**
Key difference 1		
Key difference 2		
Key difference 3		
Key difference 4		
Key difference 5		

4. Now, ask each person to call out the items on their list, and write these on a whiteboard.
5. With the group, recognise the duplications and similarities, and condense the list. Then ask the people to rank order the list, so that the most important items are assigned an A, those that are reasonably important are given a B, and the least important are rated a C.
6. Consolidate the outcomes from the four focus groups, and then invite one person from each group to another meeting to confirm the list.

You have just developed a straightforward list of the behaviours that your organisation needs if it is going to sustain a service culture.

Identify the extent to which these behaviours are present

To test the extent to which these behaviours are currently present, create a three-column table that lists the behaviours in the first column, a space for a score in the second column and the third column can be used for comments.

Table 5.2 Identifying the extent to which key management/supervisory behaviours are present

Required behaviours	**Current score**	**Comments**

Ask a sample of the customer contact people to rate their manager (anonymously of course) on a score of 1–5, with 1 meaning that the manager fully evidences this behaviour, 3 meaning that it is mostly OK, and 5 meaning that they seldom behave in this way. You can use 2 and 4 as shading. Where there are low scores, invite comments.

You have just completed a crude culture survey. You could develop it more fully if you choose, but for the moment take a look at the scores. If you have too many scores below 4, you are going to find that it is difficult to be customer oriented. If you have too many scores below 3, you are going to find it impossible.

Introduce changes if required

If you have an alarming number of low scores, then you need to do three things. The first is to review your selection criteria; you are probably choosing key people without due regard for their capacity to stimulate good service. The second is to develop a set of remedial training programmes for your managers that should be built in the same way as those for the front line – with observed behaviour and the awarding of certificates. The third is to make customer service important in your business. If your managers are not putting their time and effort into enabling the front line to deliver good service, then they must be picking up messages from somewhere that their attention should be directed elsewhere.

There are no short cuts here; if your managers are sending the wrong messages about the importance of the customer then there is no way you will be able to deliver consistently good service – no way in the world.

Reward systems

The 'employee of the month' system had taken a long time to develop. In the beginning there was the concern that while one employee was rewarded at each site, there would be many others who were not – even though they were almost as deserving. That could produce one really happy employee and dozens who resented both the individual and the process.

However, the mixture of employee and supervisor nominations, the way in which those nominations had to be supported by evidence, and the credibility of the panel that made the final selection had made the whole process challenging, credible and rewarding.

The awards were given out at a ceremony each month, which was run along the same lines as the Oscars (only much shorter, and without Billy Crystal or Whoopi Goldberg). The business had recently introduced the concept of 'selective disobedience', which is breaking the rules where necessary to create a special level of service.

This month someone who had not been nominated for 'employee of the month' was called to the stage. He was stunned that his name had been called out, and not a little concerned. He had either done something particularly brilliant, or made a terrible mistake. He rather thought that it was the latter.

The CEO looked stern. 'Let me take you back to last Tuesday,' he began in his best prosecutorial voice, 'the day when a customer asked for a product that we should have been able to provide, but which was out of stock.' A flicker of realisation rippled over the employee's face.

The CEO continued, 'You asked the customer to wait for a moment and you took an item of our stock of equivalent value off the site – without permission – and went down the road to our competitor and offered to trade that item for the one that the customer wanted. You made that trade – again without permission – and brought it back and then sold it to the customer.'

The employee looked like a rabbit caught in the headlights.

'I want to make it absolutely clear to everyone here,' boomed the CEO, 'that this is exactly the kind of selective disobedience that we have been talking about. Tonight Jason will get the inaugural "selective disobedience award".'

It was a night that Jason never forgot; it was a lesson that everyone remembered.

Talk about rewards and people immediately think about money. Sure, this is important, but many customer contact employees (outside areas connected with sales) have limited opportunity to change their levels of remuneration in the short term. There is plenty of research to suggest that once people are at work, happily engaged in tasks, money is not the critical factor in determining their performance.

There are many other forms of reward. These include:

- the way that praise is handed out;
- the way that interesting projects are allocated;
- the way that rosters are put together;
- the availability of interesting training opportunities;
- the allocation of parking spaces or other 'privileges';
- the way in which promotion criteria are constructed;
- the actual criteria used in promotions;
- the way in which managers are given positions and tasks in the organisation.

Each one of these sends a message – a powerful message. If managers in your organisation say that customer contact employees should go out of their way to satisfy a customer (even break a few rules), but the promotion process only progresses those who always comply with policy and who are never late with their paperwork, then which one are people going to listen to?

Make a list of all the different ways that people are rewarded in your organisation. Investigate what people really need to do to gain the rewards (ask the most recent recipients), and note down the behaviours that are being encouraged by your reward systems. The chances are that you will get some nasty surprises that you need to fix right away.

The way that the structure confers status

We pretend that status isn't important. We like to think that 7 million years of evolution have weakened the links between our sophisticated human society and our simian past. It isn't true.

People are finely tuned to how status is conferred – and who has it. There is the pecking order on the organisation chart, combined with many kinds of badges and symbols, from the kind of company car, to the size of the office, to the quality of the carpet.

The starting point is the organisation chart. Identify where the customer contact people are positioned. Highlight where the most senior people are who are directly identified with the work completed by those on the front line. Look for the word 'customer' in the job titles.

Now look at the remuneration structure (including cars, parking spaces, and so on), compare the different levels and see where the customer-related positions sit in the hierarchy. Rank-order the customer contact positions against the others in the same general salary band. Which appear to have the greater status in your organisation?

Now, look at all the information you have compiled. Where do the positions that deliver customer service fit? If they are the poor relations in the organisation then they will be treated as such. If this is the case, you need to look carefully at changing the way in which you are organised to deliver results.

Frontline empowerment

Frontline empowerment is ready and waiting for you right now. You only need to create the circumstances in which it can occur. There are six prerequisites to frontline empowerment:

- the right strategic intent;
- a supportive culture;
- measures that emphasise customer satisfaction;
- the right examples;

- the right people;
- training in the rules.

You will find these prerequisites overviewed in your CD ROM. Please take a moment to watch this presentation before progressing.

The right strategic intent

Empowerment is about giving more freedom, control and power to make decisions to the front line. Empowerment is not a magic answer. Empowerment is not for every organisation.

Before you can include empowerment as part of your service approach you need to be clear about the kinds of experiences that you want your customers to receive from your organisation. You need to study your customer strategy (see Chapter 3) carefully so that you can see what place a flexible front line plays in the customer experience that you have chosen to deliver for good strategic reasons.

It may be that a key way to differentiate your organisation from your competitors is to offer a noticeably different level of service, and that empowering customer contact employees is the key to making this happen. If this is the case then everyone understands what they are doing – and why – and empowerment makes sense.

On the other hand, it may emerge that your organisation needs to give exactly the same service in the same way with no capacity to vary any part of the content or the process – in which case trying to introduce empowerment is destructive.

So, take a look at your strategy. Note down the customer experience that is either stated or implied. Look at that list and assess the extent to which the front line needs to be empowered to make decisions. Develop a list of the choices that the front line can make. This is the rationale for empowerment in your organisation.

A supportive culture

'Delight the customer.' That is what Derek had been told at last week's training session. That was the new company slogan – he had the mouse mat to prove it.

Derek had done his best. He had exercised his judgement and remedied a customer complaint using the options available to him. OK, so he had combined a couple of options together, but wasn't the point of all this to give him the freedom to respond to unique customers in unique situations?

Now Derek was confused. His supervisor said that these were the kinds of decisions that Derek should have referred upwards. There had been a terse note from accounts asking why a credit note had been raised. Derek looked to his fellow customer contact people. They shrugged their shoulders – no one knew what he had done wrong.

What do you think will happen to frontline empowerment in Derek's organisation? It hasn't got a snowball's chance in hell.

There is no point in introducing a range of options and choices for customer contact people if the prevailing attitude is to take all decisions to the supervisory levels, and if people at the front line are punished if they use their power to make decisions. Too many organisations introduce empowerment by training the people at the front line in new behaviours. In most cases these behaviours are obvious; it is the existing culture that needs to be dismantled so that empowered behaviour is permitted.

Ask yourself this question: 'Why don't we have the level of empowerment that we want?' Now list the reasons under headings:

- supervisors' attitudes and behaviour;
- rules that prohibit empowered behaviour (look at the immediate frontline rules as well as accounting, risk management, property, insurance, legal, and so on);
- the prevailing attitudes of your customer contact people;
- provision of skills, resources and reward systems that facilitate empowerment.

This simple question will show you what needs to be addressed before you can begin to talk about empowerment.

If you want to generate more in-depth information, a well-designed culture survey will provide you with the information that you need. If you do not have the time for a major survey, another way to collect some very interesting information about the prevailing attitudes in your business is to analyse the two characteristics that have a big impact on culture: fear and freedom.

Fear

Fear is a primary driver of human behaviour. To a greater or lesser extent we are all defined by our fears. Add a little fear into an organisation and people stop taking chances, they spend more time diluting responsibility in meetings, and they introduce lots of checking steps.

If the fear persists (for years) then people become increasingly uncomfortable with even minor change. They displace anxiety in lots of activities that were never high priority – such as developing complex policies for incredibly obvious problems – and they produce few ideas about how to change the situation.

Build an organisation with low levels of fear and you will see the opposite. Here you will find creativity, limited use of hierarchy to get things done, all kinds of attempts to make changes, and probably some genuine breakthroughs.

Ask 10 people (from different levels in your organisation) in two focus group sessions of 45 minutes each the following questions:

- What are people afraid of in this organisation (losing their jobs, making a mistake, not getting pay increases, their managers, irate customers, etc)?
- How rational is that fear?
- How does that fear affect their behaviour?
- To what extent have the current managers developed this fear?

Within the answers to these simple questions are some of the insights that will help you to understand how the tone you set as a manager affects what people do every day. However, be very careful when you answer these questions, because culture is difficult to see from within. Ask someone who has just joined as well as someone who has just left to get some different perspectives.

Freedom

Organisations are complex. In an empowered business, people from supervisory levels upwards need to have the freedom to work within fairly broad guidelines so that they can get the outcomes required.

To be able to confer this freedom an organisation needs to be confident that it has the right people, the right information systems to support their decision making and the right feedback systems to ensure that everything does not go off the rails. This freedom is only possible when there is a mixture of good design and interpersonal trust.

When people have this freedom they find ways around day-to-day problems. When the freedom is absent then too many decisions are bounded by rules – which can never cover all circumstances – and so too many decisions end up in the in-trays of senior managers and do nothing but gobble up their time and slow the whole organisation down.

The level of freedom available is easy to assess: just look at the restrictions imposed by the rules and levels of delegated authority. Interview five supervisors and ask them to describe the limits placed on their decision making, and what they could accomplish if their freedom were increased.

Once you are clear about the degree of fear and the levels of freedom, prepare two one-page reports. The first report should show the results of the fear focus groups. You should list the key findings for each group for each question. The second report should show the restrictions placed on decision making, with conclusions about the appropriateness of those limits.

You are now ready to place your organisation on the 'fear–freedom' matrix (Figure 5.2).

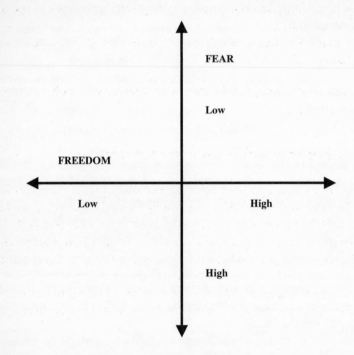

Figure 5.2   The fear–freedom culture analysis matrix

Take a look at your findings. Assess the answers for the freedom data on a scale that shows 'High' freedom (fully responsible and able to make all necessary decisions), 'Medium' (key decisions not available), and 'Low' (needs to refer even the most trivial decisions). Then assess the degree of fear on a three-point scale: high, medium and low. (High means that people are afraid of making changes, offering ideas, holding a different viewpoint from their manager, and are concerned about losing their job. Low means that there is little use of hierarchical power, everyone feels safe to express their views and experiment with new ways to achieve results, and they feel that their jobs are secure. Medium is in between.)

Now, place your organisation on the four-quadrant scale. Your position on the quadrant tells you what shared behaviours are likely to be present in your organisation:

- Low fear + high freedom = innovative, accepting of change, experimental.
- Low fear + low freedom = frustration, challenges to authority, rules will be broken.
- High fear + high freedom = upward delegation, meetings to share decisions, low innovation.
- High fear + low freedom = dependence on rules and precedents, resistance to change.

This straightforward analysis will show you whether your culture is compatible with empowerment.

Measures that emphasise customer satisfaction

Empowerment carries a number of risks. There is the probability of inconsistency, the likelihood that some mistakes will be made, and the possibility that some costs will be incurred that otherwise might have been avoided.

The pay-off is seen in increased customer satisfaction. However, if your measurement systems are good at tracking inconsistency, mistakes and costs and they are poor at assessing customer satisfaction – then empowerment is going to look like a huge mistake. Make sure that you have good satisfaction measures (see Chapter 9) if you want to successfully introduce and sustain frontline empowerment.

The right examples

We all learn by watching, before we learn by doing. Those in customer contact positions will watch two groups of people:

- the managers/supervisors;
- those on the same level doing the same kind of work.

The managers/supervisors

Frontline empowerment is a gift. It is the gift of power and control given by managers/supervisors to those who work for them. The recipients need to be sure that it has been permanently conferred.

The chances are that people on the front line are going to be at best cautious and at worst sceptical when they are given some new freedom. They are going to be watching for the signs that the managers/supervisors have changed their minds. This means that the managers/supervisors have to be particularly careful about how they behave. If a frontline person asks a supervisor to make a decision that should really be made at the front line then the supervisor needs to say something like, *'Talk me through your options. . . tell me which one you think is the best and why. . . and now go ahead and do it.'* The supervisor needs to be very careful that they do not give the answer – otherwise they will spend the rest of their time suffering with the front line delegating straightforward decisions upwards (which is a form of pretend managing – see Chapter 4).

Those on the same level doing the same kind of work

There will be some people who are naturally good at exercising the freedom that empowerment confers. You need to watch out for these people, and catch them at the moment when they behave in exactly the right way. You can then reward that individual's behaviour with praise (so that they will continue) and remind everyone else that this is the kind of way they should all be responding to customers, either through others having seen you giving the praise, or by using that real example as a story to tell in your next team meeting.

So, by stopping managers/supervisors from setting the wrong example, and by rewarding those on the front line who set the right example, you create the live models for people to follow.

The right people

In the previous chapter we looked at the characteristics that make up good customer contact employees. Basically, if your front line does not have a reasonable representation of all these characteristics then customer service is going to be elusive. Empowerment will be nearly impossible.

If you conclude that you need to reshape the profile of your people then do so before you try to introduce empowerment.

Training in the rules

So, you have a clear strategic reason for empowering the front line, the culture is sympathetic, the measurement systems can describe the benefits, the right examples are in place, and the right people are ready to take the decisions available. You are ready for empowerment. In fact, you already have an empowered front line; all they need from you now are the rules.

Your empowerment training should be about these rules. You have two main options: 'structured empowerment' and 'unstructured empowerment'.

Structured empowerment

Structured empowerment means that the rules are defined for different situations. So, for example, in a restaurant a dissatisfied customer can be offered a complimentary meal, or a bottle of wine, or a voucher for another meal on another day. The frontline person can choose the best solution. The thought in the employee's mind is, *'Which option will provide the greatest benefit to the customer?'*

Unstructured empowerment

Unstructured empowerment means that the frontline person has a budget, and can use his or her discretion. In the same example the frontline person may have a £200 limit to work within. He or she can complement the meal, maybe offer a night's accommodation if the restaurant is attached to a hotel, offer a gift, and so on. The thought in the employee's mind is, *'What can I do to make this right for the customer?'*

All the hotel employees know that each guest spends an average of 20 nights a year with them. They know that the lifetime value of each customer runs into the hundreds of thousands of pounds. They know that a lot is at stake every time a guest complains.

If a customer has a problem, the hotel wants it to be fixed – right away, by the person who is first notified by that guest.

Each frontline person has a budget of £2,000. They can provide any kind of compensation (free night, meals, room hire, and so on) that they think will satisfy the guest within that limit. If they need a greater level of compensation then a frontline person can join with another frontline person and they can combine limits, giving them a total of £4,000. If that is not enough, they can enlist another frontline person, and so on, and all this without any reference to a supervisor.

One time the whole night shift clubbed together to compensate 50 wedding guests. The management was delighted.

The kind of empowerment that you need will depend on your organisation and your strategic intent. Whichever one you use, you need to be sure that the rules are clear.

So, you have created a culture that has the capacity to deliver outcomes, and you have inserted an empowered front line into that culture (if that matches your strategic intent). Now that you have attended to the customer and employee aspects of service it is time to consider the processes and infrastructure that you need to produce the outcomes that you want. These are covered in the next chapters.

6

Using the positive power
of complaints

The day had not gone according to plan. The room was not ready, the meal was no better than ordinary, and the deputy assistant manager was more than unhelpful – he was the modern-day Basil Fawlty of the motel business.

Peter hated any kind of conflict, confrontation or complaint. He would rather smile politely and never come back. But this was too much. He asked to see the manager.

Here is a golden moment for the owners of the motel. They have the chance to learn something important about their processes and people. They are in a position to create a story that Peter will tell for months if they recover successfully. They are about to receive a gift.

What are the chances that the manager will see Peter's complaint in that way? Not good.

It is more than likely that the complaint will be treated as an insult, and that the motel owner will try to prove that Peter is wrong. That will create an entirely different story – a story that will drive business away. The kind of story that is like toothpaste – once it is out of the tube you can never put it back.

The problem is that complaints have got a bad reputation – one they do not deserve. People hide them, avoid them, ignore them and blame the person who generated the complaint in the first place. This is crazy.

Customers switch to a competitor when they are dissatisfied. The percentages differ from study to study, but it is entirely possible that only 4 per cent of customers complain. That means for every complaint you receive, there were another 26 people who were unhappy, but did not tell you. Of those who are unhappy, it is possible that 65 per cent (or more) will never buy from you again. Not only that, these disgruntled customers will tell 10 (or more) of their friends or colleagues about their experience. It is probable that some of these people will retell the experience – and so the bad stories multiply.

Complaints offer you three benefits:

- free research;
- the opportunity to improve broken processes;
- the chance to recover – and create a story.

These are covered on the CD ROM that accompanies this book. If you can, have a look at the presentation on your CD ROM before continuing.

Free research

It is the customers who eat the meals, sit in the seats, use the equipment, deal with the frontline staff, receive the services, read the instruction manuals, make the products work, sleep in the beds, wait for the representatives to arrive, apply the advice, and find as many ways as they can to extract – and add – value to your products/services.

They know more about what it is like to do business with your organisation than you do. They know when things go wrong far sooner than you can, and they understand the effect of a breakdown more clearly than you will.

Sometimes – not always – but sometimes they tell someone in your organisation. You could not conduct research that was this sensitive, you could not buy information this precious. You should not waste any of it.

There are three steps you need to take to make sure that you gain the greatest advantage from your complaints. These are:

- Stimulate complaints.
- Create a 'do not walk past' attitude.
- Capture the data.

Stimulate complaints

When is a complaint a complaint? This is an interesting question. What does it mean when a customer asks, *'Have you ever thought about having bedside lamps?'* or makes a comment such as *'The other place I stayed in provided tea-and coffee-making facilities.'* Are these complaints? Are they the way that some people like to package an expression of dissatisfaction? How are these bits of information treated in your organisation?

The chances are that your customer contact people hear lots of comments, observations and suggestions that are never registered as complaints, and which far outweigh the number of 'red-faced yelling events' commonly associated with a dissatisfied customer. The chances are that most of this information is lost.

The bottom line is – it doesn't matter how information comes to your business, it should *all* be treated as part of the research process that makes your organisation stronger. Taking that a step further, this information should be deliberately stimulated. Take the word 'complaint' (which is too emotion laden to be much use anymore) out of your vocabulary and start to talk about 'free research'.

Now start to get as much of this free research as possible. This means asking different questions.

Right now, someone is being asked, *'Was everything all right?'* The inevitable reply is, *'Yes, it was very nice, thank you'* – even when it wasn't. It is a ritual that is sustained by frontline people who do not really want the truth, and perpetuated by customers who do not want the hassle. It may happen as often as a million times a day.

Try a different question: *'Could you tell me one thing we could do better next time?'* Imagine what people will say. Imagine how many ideas you would collect by the end of the week. Imagine how many improvements you could make in the next 12 months. Many of your complaints will be netted up by this question – so they will be seen as part of the research process.

It is so easy, and all it takes is the right attitude

Create a 'do not walk past' attitude

People will fear complaints when they feel that they will be punished. This fear will contaminate your organisation if you let it. It may even contribute to the demise of your business.

You need to create a 'do not walk past' attitude. This is when people are keenly aware of the fact that most problems are caused by the process, not the people, and that everyone is involved in collecting free research. The ingredients of this attitude are as follows:

Most problems are caused by the process, not the people

We like to reduce problems to the individual level. We like to be able to find people to blame if things go wrong. It is human nature. It isn't how organisations really work.

In most organisations almost all of the problems are caused by a process or system that is imperfectly designed or improperly functioning. The more data you have about the problems, the easier it is to analyse the root causes and weed them out. Of course there are mistakes. We all make them, but in the overall picture these represent a small percentage of the things that go wrong.

Once you make it clear that you are not looking for individuals to blame, but rather for the systemic root causes, there will be a much greater willingness to be involved in collecting and analysing the data generated by free research.

Everyone is involved in collecting free research

Customers will not go out of their way to find the right person if they have a comment/suggestion/complaint. They will tell whomever they come into contact with. Therefore everyone needs to be ready to thank the customer for his or her comments, and own the problem of making sure that the concern will be actioned. This reaction to free research should be made clear in the induction training, reinforced by what managers say, and modelled on what managers do.

Once everyone understands that this is part of their job, all they need is a central place to capture the data.

Capture the data

People who analyse data like to have as much of it as possible, at the greatest level of detail. The front line who are responsible for providing the data like to be able to do so as quickly and simply as possible. There is tension here.

The mistake is to let the data analyst develop the forms and procedures – they will be disconcerting in their design, annoying in the analysis required, and daunting in the details. You will get a better result if you let customer contact people create the design in conjunction with the person who needs to make sense of it all and produce the reports.

The simplest way to capture the required data is to have a straightforward card or e-mail form where the basic details can be entered. This can then be sent, or dropped into a central point where it is recorded, and then the person who provided it can be thanked. When the data are used to review process change, the person who sent in those data should be notified, and informed again when the resulting change is to be implemented. People will continue to go out of their way to give you data if you let them know that their effort is appreciated and has made a difference.

The opportunity to improve broken processes

The airline carried millions of passengers every year. A competitor could just as easily service each one of those passengers. The airline was determined to do whatever it could to keep its customers coming back again and again. It wanted all the free research it could get.

Employees were encouraged to ask the 'Tell us the one thing we could do better?' kinds of questions; passengers were given the opportunity to call through their thoughts/suggestions/complaints on a hotline; a specific complaints unit was available to passengers 24 hours a day.

All the information collected was coded and analysed. Every month a list of complaints was produced and sorted by frequency. The complaint at the top of the list was given to a team to further analyse and then remedy. The team had one instruction: 'Do what it takes to make this complaint go away.' The team could interview as many customers as they needed to, they could fly to any country, they could trial new equipment or processes. The effectiveness of their solution was easy to measure: if the complaints reduced and then evaporated, the team had done its job. If the complaints stayed at the top of the list, the team kept on working.

There are two reasons why you need to research and change your processes – a) they do not work as they are supposed to, and/or b) the processes still work as they were designed to, but the customers' needs and expectations have changed.

In either case, suggestions/complaints offer the opportunity to identify what is going wrong – and fix it. There are four straightforward steps:

- Select the timeframe.
- Analyse the data.
- Analyse the broken processes.
- Fix the processes.

Select the timeframe

If you are a business that has huge volumes of transactions every day then you need to look at your free research every day – you cannot afford to carry a broken process. This means generating reports that capture what customers have said every 24 hours. If your business has longer cycle times and slower progressions of activities then you may be able to do the analysis every week, or even every month. Work out how long it will take for you to identify a trend that signals a problem in your organisation, and use this as your time interval.

Analyse the data

Create two rank order lists of the suggestions/complaints that you have collected within your timeframe. On the first list, record the frequency of the suggestions/complaints, with the most frequent at the top of the list. On the second list, rank-order the financial impact that the process problem identified by the suggestion/complaint is having on your organisation, again with the largest impact at the top of the list.

Put the two lists next to each other, and highlight the items that represent the greatest impact and the highest volumes. These are the items that need to be addressed first. Pick no more than the top three to work on, and make sure that the problem is fully resolved before moving to items further down the list.

Analyse the broken processes

The analysis you have completed so far has shown what is going wrong, but it has not told you why. To find this out, you need to analyse the processes that gave rise to the problem. This involves process mapping.

Essentially, you should keep three thoughts in mind when looking at customer service process problems:

- The 80:20 rule works. You will find that around 80% of the problems within a service process are caused by 20% of that process.
- Observation is your most powerful way to get a rapid insight into what is really going on. As described earlier in this book, if you sit quietly and unobtrusively with a clear mind and a fresh eye and watch what people do to produce the problem that you are investigating, then in more than 50% of the cases you will know the root cause within two days.
- The people on the front line probably know what is going wrong. If you convene some focus groups and ask them to concentrate on the items on your list and then ask them what they find frustrating, what improvements they would make and how they think the problem arose, you will probably get enough insight to be able to develop some remedial programmes.

Fix the processes

Typically, when the causes of a broken process are clear, the remedial action is pretty obvious. There are three steps that you need to complete:

- Gain commitment.
- Develop a good plan.
- Get started.

Gain commitment

Change in organisations is never easy. Change happens when senior people insist that – in spite of all the obstacles – the outcome required will be achieved. You need to be sure that a senior person is willing to put some weight behind the required process changes.

Develop a good plan

It may seem obvious, but too often the behavioural outcomes required are not properly defined, and so the plan is a set of changes that will not necessarily deliver the outcomes. You should test your plan by asking four questions:

- How does this plan resolve the identified problems?
- When will this plan deliver the required changes?
- What business measurement will be affected, and by how much?
- Specifically, what frontline and/or management behaviour change will this plan produce?

If your plan can survive uninhibited scrutiny using these questions, you have a better than average chance of success.

Get started

It can be tempting to wait for the right time, or to hold back until some extra details arrive, or to see what happens with a possible product launch, or restructure, or merger. . . or whatever. There is always a reason to delay, and never a perfect time.

Getting started is often the stumbling block. You should treat what you are doing as urgent right from the beginning, and get started as soon as possible.

The chance to recover – and create a story

Here is a strange fact: you will create a stronger relationship with a customer who experiences a problem followed by a good recovery than you will if you never have a problem at all. Also, the recovery will make a powerful story that will define the kind of organisation that you represent. It is likely to be repeated up to 10 times.

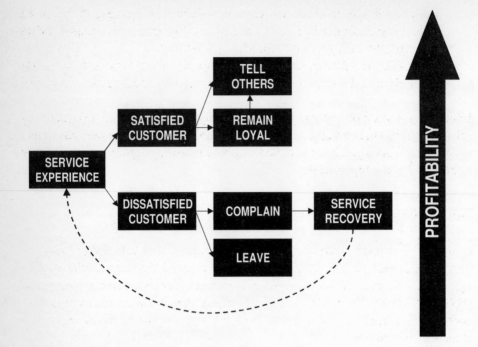

Figure 6.1   The power of good recovery

However, there is a downside. If you do not recover quickly and effectively, you can lose the lifetime value of that customer's business, along with any business that he or she may turn away from your organisation. That can be a lot of money.

The more clearly your business understands how much money, the more likely it is that managers and those on the front line will take both customer service and complaints management seriously. There are two calculations that you should perform: the effect on total profits, and the lifetime value of a single customer.

The effect on total profits

You need the following information:

- total sales;
- total number of customers;
- number of customers lost each year;

- the percentage of those lost customers who left because they had an unhappy experience (you will need to mix together your complaint data with frontline insights and produce a guesstimate);
- the impact on sales (making some assumptions about your customers – do you only lose the small ones, are all customers of equal value, and so on).

Using this information you can calculate the impact of 'unhappy experiences' on sales. You could then add this to the cost of wooing and winning new customers to replace the ones you have lost, and combine these two figures. You are likely to be looking at a big number.

The lifetime value of a customer

Consider an average customer and count the number and value of transactions they conduct each year. Produce a total annual figure. Now consider the average age of your customers, and the number of years that they typically buy your products/services. Work out the typical amount that the average customer will spend in their lifetime of doing business with you. For many organisations this is another big number.

Make sure that everyone who is likely to be involved in any kind of recovery activity knows these numbers intimately. Whenever they initiate a recovery sequence they should be aware that they are preserving this amount for your organisation.

The recovery strategy

Once frontline people fully understand the financial consequences of losing a customer they will approach the whole issue of recovery from a completely different point of view. Recovery strategies vary from organisation to organisation. The general rules are as follows:

- Thank the person for bringing the problem to your attention.
- Act fast. Often the customer just wants to receive an acknowledgement that something has gone wrong – and will now be put right.
- Make sure that the frontline staff know what to do.
- Provide a benefit to the customer that is sufficient to 'make it right' in their mind – which means they will get a benefit that is beyond their previous expectations.

These simple steps will reduce the impact of a complaint, and boost your ability to retain your customer's business and goodwill.

So, what we have covered is a major shift in the way that complaints are treated and managed in your organisation. Once they are actively sought as free research, and once real and meaningful process change is seen to be the outcome of collecting information, you will have the chance to improve your organisation in ways that you only ever imagined. These changes can be incorporated in your service design and layout, a subject that is covered in the next chapter.

7

Making it all work

Businesses like McDonald's are so successful because they work. They work because they have the processes and infrastructure that support success. This chapter describes the key concepts and frameworks that managers need to apply to design an organisation so that it can deliver the best outcomes for your business and your customers. This chapter covers three areas:

- service processes;
- service functionality and design;
- process improvement.

Service processes

James had just broken up with his girlfriend. The break-up was ugly and hostile, and James was bruised to his soul. He needed to do something to restore his capacity to feel joy again – to feel anything again. He needed to rebuild his self-esteem. He considered a move to another city, an expensive holiday, a completely new wardrobe, a sports car. He settled on a haircut.

He chose the newest, most exclusive, most expensive hair specialist in town – The Clipping Room. Right from the start the Clipping Room experience was different. When

James rang to make an appointment, a voice message asked him to use his keypad to 'Press 1 for a cut and style appointment, press 2 for a colour or perm. . .'. He made his selection and was given a number which he was asked to quote when he came in the following Saturday. This was more like booking an airline ticket than remodelling the hairy end of his body.

When he arrived, he keyed his number into a computer and took a seat. He didn't have to wait long for the experience to begin. One person washed his hair. Another dried and combed it. The hairstylist then read the computer request and gave him a series of style options. The hair was then cut and styled in silence before a fourth person dried off the hair. Finally, James was returned to reception to pay.

Coming out of the salon, James should have been both physically altered and psychologically soothed. The truth was that he felt disappointed. The haircut was OK, but it wasn't really what he had hoped for. Something was missing about the whole experience, but he couldn't quite put his finger on it. That would be his one and only visit to the exotic world of The Clipping Room.

What went wrong with this service experience? As you read through this chapter you will learn about the different types of service processes and their elements, and this will make it considerably easier to understand where The Clipping Room's processes are poorly defined and how they could be improved. The two key components to understand are 'service process elements' (key components of the process) and the 'types of service processes' (what is actually being processed and how this affects the service design)

Service process elements

There are three elements to any service process. These are:

- inputs;
- outputs;
- supplementary services.

Inputs

Inputs are elements that go into the process. Think about inputs as elements that need something to be *done* to them. In the case of The Clipping Room the input is James's current hairstyle and his need for self-esteem. From this mindset, the next question becomes obvious: *what* is it we need to do to them?

As simple as it may seem, this way of looking at the service will define the service promise. It will also help determine the ideal service configuration –

including where the service should be located, how it should be laid out, what resources are needed and what the service should look like to the customer.

Outputs

Outputs are what the service produces. In the case of the hairstylist, the output is not only the haircut, but also the 'feel good' emotions that go with that. In other words, the output is a physical transformation as well as a psychological one.

Outputs are judged by the customer on two levels: a) on the technical quality (how good the hair cut is); and also b) on the functional quality (ie how efficient was the process; how friendly was the service, etc). Often the latter can be influenced by the business's choice of supplementary services.

Supplementary services

Supplementary services are the services offered that are designed to support the core service. So, what other service does the average hairstylist offer in delivering to this core need? The typical hairstyling salon might offer complimentary tea or coffee; magazines or forms of entertainment; styling or colouring advice, etc. The whole package of offerings is therefore shown below – with the supplementary services supporting the *way* in which the core need is fulfilled.

Figure 7.1 Basic supplementary services for a hair salon

But it is even more subtle than this. There are three aspects of these supplementary services that need to be understood and managed:

- people processing;
- materials processing;
- information processing.

People processing

People processing involves any service in which people or customers (individually or collectively) are the inputs. Although it sounds a pretty crude way of looking at a service, this is exactly what is happening – people have an expectation (some of which is unspoken) to be transformed in some way, whether it is a physical, mental, emotional or spiritual transformation (see Chapter 1). Think about the following services and the types of transformations that take place:

- hairstyling – physical transformation (haircut); psychological transformation (self-esteem);
- university education – physical transformation (a certificate); mental transformation (learning); psychological transformation (confidence);
- palm-reading – physical transformation (a chart); spiritual transformation (sense of certainty about the future).

What about the service you offer? Are you 'processing people'? If so, be sure that you understand the required outputs and the types of supplementary services that will generally support delivery of these outputs. Complete Table 7.1.

Table 7.1 Table to identify the transformation your customers require

Service	Physical transformation	Mental transformation	Emotional transformation	Spiritual transformation	Implication for supplementary services

These are not easy data to uncover. You will need to observe your customers and use techniques like the 'corridor technique' (described in Chapter 3 in the section on focus groups). You will probably find that people are looking for many 'pay-offs' from your business that you need to satisfy deliberately.

Materials processing

Materials processing involves changing something that belongs to the customer in a way that provides a benefit (or at least you hope it does). Types of outputs in these cases include solutions or repairs, physical enhancement or change in physical form. Examples are:

- mechanical repairs – solution (repair of brakes);
- interior decorating – physical enhancement of environment;
- building services – transformation of timber and steel into housing.

Services that process materials are becoming more and more common as supplementary offers of retailing outlets. Local video stores offer video service repairs; computer stores repair computers; and so on.

If the core service you are offering customers involves processing their assets or materials, then the types of supplementary services to offer will include benefits such as pick-up and/or delivery; regular information updates or progress reports; installation and warranties. If you provide these, make sure that they meet your customers' physical, mental, emotional or spiritual needs (see the comments on a 'people processing service' below, and see Chapter 1).

Information processing

Information processing involves the core service taking information as its input and transforming it into either a new physical form or an intangible asset. For example:

- accounting – transforming information into a tax return;
- consulting – transforming information into a business plan or market advice;
- market research – transforming data into brand or business strategies.

In these cases, the supplementary services include some form of professional documentation, prompt and accurate billing, problem resolution or supplementary advice. They also rely on a high level of personalised interaction to enable the core service to be completed.

So, with all this in mind, let's go back for a moment, and reflect on the Clipping Room case and what made James uncomfortable with the service. Take a moment to analyse what may have gone wrong.

You have probably worked out what the fated Clipping Room has done. It goes back to James's expectations, which were moulded by his past experiences with hairstylists. You see, when customers make an appointment for a haircut (as James did), they typically speak with someone on the phone, not to a machine. When they enter a hair salon, they are usually treated in a friendly and personalised way – not as an 'input' to be moved through a process.

The problem, fundamentally, was that The Clipping Room, in searching for efficiencies, had forgotten that the core service they offered was a *people processing service*. In doing so, they had designed a service that may have delivered to the core need of the customer (a haircut), but failed to deliver to some of the other needs of the customer such as self-esteem or sense of belonging (after all, isn't the head massage the best part of the experience for many people?). Clearly, the lack of personalised treatment and two-way interaction let the customer down.

The key learning – particularly for those who are designing a new way to deliver a service – is that when you are designing your service, you must reflect on *what* it is that is being processed (ie what the inputs are), what the required outputs are (functional and emotional needs), and what supplementary services fit best with the type of service process you intend to offer.

Service functionality and design

Roy was truly impressed as he walked through the hotel foyer to the reception area. He had never stayed in such a smart-looking hotel before. He paused for a moment to appreciate the marble waterfall. This was going to be an experience to remember.

As he approached the reception area, however, his initial reactions began to change. A crowd of guests were waiting to check in. They had clearly been there for a while, and their expressions told the story of frustration and disappointment. Overstretched receptionists bumped into each other as they tried to solve queries about bills as well as complete the check-in procedures. It was a shambles.

Now Roy was less impressed. He noticed that his girlfriend's smile had turned into a frown. This was the first memory of his special holiday, and it wasn't a good one.

You probably remember very little about your last visit to the bank. . . except, perhaps, how long you had to stand in a queue. Or the last time you visited a large department store or shopping centre. . . unless you were pushed for time and desperate to get to a meeting.

Most businesses are designed to look attractive to the customer. What is often overlooked is the functionality of the service. This is not to say that décor and image are not important. Of course they are. In many cases they define the business and contribute to its positioning in the customer's mind. However, due consideration needs to be given to providing the right balance between looking appealing and delivering to the customer's needs.

Service functionality

Service functionality refers to the way in which the business is designed to ensure that the service is delivered in the best possible way. There are two aspects to service functionality: 'service efficiency' and 'customer efficiency'.

Service efficiency

Service efficiency is all about designing the business so that it is easy for employees to serve customers. Take the example of the immaculate hotel foyer. It was clearly beautiful and extravagantly expensive, but all of that was over-shadowed by the problems at the reception desk. In this particular case, there were two elements of service inefficiency:

- The computerised check-in system was at the other end of reception from where the keys were kept (approximately 3 metres away).
- The reception counter was used for customer queries and complaints, but no queuing system had been implemented.

Only two small oversights in design, but two oversights that resulted in the following costly impacts:

- Check-in time was longer.
- The perception of a crowd was created.
- The area in front of reception was difficult to keep clean, as it was always busy.
- The carpeted area behind reception was worn out with undue traffic and had to be replaced within six months of the hotel opening.
- Staff became frustrated with heavy demand (as well as bumping into one another behind reception). Staff complaints and turnover in reception began to climb.

In a moment, we will talk about what you can do to make sure your business is designed to maximise service efficiency. First, however, we need to reflect on the other side of the coin, too: customer efficiency.

Customer efficiency

Customer efficiency is about how efficiently customers learn about your service and interact with you in the most efficient way. Often, efficient interaction will require navigation around your premises. Sometimes it will mean knowing the best way to contact you or to access information.

Consider the following questions (using one or several of the research techniques covered in Chapter 2):

- Is it easy for customers to find your business?
- Is it easy for customers to find the amenities?
- Is the process logical for customers to use? (For example, do customers 'jump the queue' without knowing it?)
- Can customers move about freely without being impeded by furniture, fittings or other customers?
- Is it easy for customers to find or ask for help?
- Do customers know your business hours?
- Do they know where to park and how to access your business after hours?

If the answer to any of these questions is 'no', then you are losing business.

You need to provide both service efficiency (from your point of view) and customer efficiency (from their point of view). You need to take both into consideration when you create the following four key areas for your business:

- the service blueprint;
- service layouts;
- capacity management;
- the role of physical products.

The service blueprint

Imagine someone is going to build you a new home. Before they begin construction, you will obviously want to see an architectural plan of what the house will look like. After all, it's no use building the house and then debating which direction the kitchen should be facing.

Designing a service is no different from building a house. Before the development phase, you will need a clear plan of how the service is to be offered and what the business will look like – from a tangible as well as a process perspective.

This service blueprint fulfils the same role. It is the same as an architectural blueprint that spells out the design of the service, breaking it down into separate, yet interrelated components.

Even though a service blueprint is most relevant to new, developing services, you will also find it beneficial to draw one up now. Chances are that you will be surprised at just how service is delivered in your business, and the blueprint will give you the foundations that you need to begin some process improvement. To create a blueprint, work through these five steps:

1. Identify all the components of a service process that staff need to perform. List each of these.
2. Now draw each of these components as a flow diagram so they are in the desired order, with arrows showing the flow from one stage to another. Figure 7.2 shows a simplified chart of a check-in process.

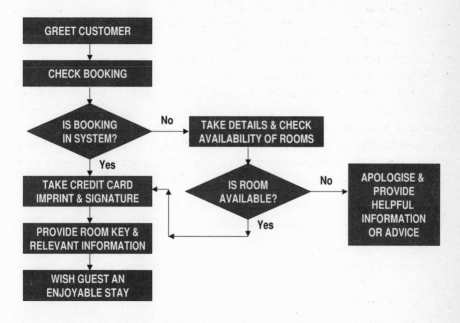

Figure 7.2   An example of a service process: check-in

3. Now calculate the time it takes to complete each of these steps to establish an appropriate service standard.
4. Identify the most likely '*strangle-points*' in the process – that is, the elements of the process where activities come together and that are most likely to throw the whole system out of sync or into disarray. These will form priorities for maintenance, training and process improvement within the organisation (eg computer failure, bookings not entered correctly, etc).

5. Finally, consider the tangible aspects of the business. What do you need the facilities to look like to ensure that this process works properly (ie a computerised booking system at reception; credit card machines on hand; room keys close by; etc)?

Developing a service blueprint is important in several ways. First, it provides a clear definition of the service component, as well as the role of the service employee. Second, it allows development of realistic service standards. Third, it highlights potential 'strangle-points', so that systems can be designed to maintain flow. Finally, the service blueprint helps you to lay out a work area that minimises staff movement and maximises staff efficiency.

Service layouts

Lucy wanted to treat her parents to a nice dinner for their wedding anniversary. They had worked hard all their lives, and they had 'done it tough'. Eating out was an extravagance they could seldom afford, and they had never been to a restaurant that had tablecloths.

She chose an expensive restaurant and made a booking for 7 pm. Arriving a little earlier than anticipated in the unaccustomed luxury of a taxi, Lucy was politely informed that their table was not quite ready and they would have to wait. A warming drink at the bar might have been a pleasant start to the evening, but there was no bar. In fact, there was nowhere to wait at all.

After they had been standing in the street for 20 minutes the novelty of watching the wind twist the falling snow into interesting patterns had worn off, and Lucy and her parents were very glad to be shown to their table. The blackboard menu was pointed out to them, but Lucy's father could only see the entrées because the rest of the menu was obstructed by one of the large pillars in the restaurant area. Lucy's mother had a better line of sight, but the combination of the dim lighting and the spidery chalk writing left her less enlightened than her husband.

Lucy spent some time describing the menu – time that she had intended to use for conversation and reminiscing. She hoped that once the order was placed there would be time for celebrating what so many years of marriage had meant to the family. It didn't go as planned. Light-hearted chatter turned into polite wondering about when the meal would arrive, which transformed into grumbling about 'how long does it take to cook a bit of fish', which resulted in a rather embarrassing complaint.

The food arrived just as the restaurant was filling up, and several times during the course of their meal, Lucy felt the person sitting behind her bump into her chair. One impact made her spill her red wine on her white dress – not a good combination. Looking more closely, she noticed that the table behind them was particularly close to theirs – probably because that table was far too big for the space it was meant to occupy.

In the taxi on the way home Lucy's mother thanked her for the thought, but suggested that next time they should go to the local Indian restaurant, which served excellent food and did so quickly and efficiently. She was sure that Sanjay would allow them to bring a tablecloth. Lucy was disappointed in her mother's reaction, but had to acknowledge that she was right – the local restaurant would have been much better.

Lucy was never going to have an excellent experience in this restaurant, even though the food was world class. There were several conditions that worked against both efficiency and customer comfort in the restaurant. These included:

- While internal pillars were part of the fixed premises, and therefore difficult to change, the restaurant had not used the pillars to best advantage.
- The choice of table styles and sizes and the seating layout used contributed to the sense of calamity, rather than creating an appropriate ambience.
- The kitchen design was even worse, making efficiency nearly impossible to achieve.

The layout of facilities is as important to service organisations as it is to large manufacturers. Have you ever wondered why, in some restaurants (particularly those that provide fast food), you stand in a queue to place your order, while in others the waiter or waitress will come to you to take your order? Have you ever moved into a new office building and wondered what the rationale was behind the layout of the new environment? The chances are that a considerable amount of thought has gone into those layouts. The layout of the facilities is critical for three different reasons:

- It can affect the technical quality of the service (ie the outputs).
- It can affect the functional quality of the service (ie the way in which the output is delivered).
- It can affect customer perceptions of the service.

There are complex models and methods to determine the ideal layout. However, you will be able to improve your layout dramatically if you make two key distinctions.

The two key distinctions
At the most fundamental level, there are two key types of service layouts to choose from: 1) product-based layouts and 2) process-based layouts. Both should be applied to meet four key objectives:

- Minimise the cost of materials handling and movement.
- Minimise the probability of congestion and delay.
- Maximise the utilisation of capacity, facilities and labour (minimise wastage).
- Ensure that customer perceptions are in line with organisational objectives.

Product-based layouts Product-based layouts are those where activities are arranged in a sequence and customers move through the activities in that sequence. When you visit a supermarket, you encounter a product-based layout: the fruit and vegetables are in one section; bakery items in a separate section and pet food in yet another part of the supermarket. More importantly, customers are encouraged to proceed around the service in a systematic manner so that they encounter the entire service without missing any stage of it.

If your service is highly standardised (eg a fast food outlet), if it is important that customers move through stages of it in sequence (eg a car wash), or you want to make sure that customers don't 'miss' any part of it (eg a museum or art gallery), a product-based layout is right for you.

Process-based layouts A process-based layout is where the technology or skill base of the organisation is critical to the business design. In these situations, customers generally use the service by choosing to interact with only one aspect of the entire service offering.

Take a hospital, for instance – the hospital is designed most efficiently when the different services are separated into different wards – paediatrics, maternity, cardiology, oncology, etc. If your service requires highly professional sets of skills (eg a university), if a high degree of personalisation is required to service a customer (eg medicine), and if customers are likely to only require one part of a much broader offering (eg department store), a process-based layout is the right choice.

Use the checklist shown in Table 7.2 to select the best kind of layout for your business.

Service design

When designing your service, you need to consider two areas: 'capacity management' and 'the role of physical product'.

Capacity management

Most businesses have a capacity level that is fixed. Sure, the manager can call in casual staff where necessary to deal with periods of high demand, but the

Table 7.2 Choosing a product-based or service-based approach

Consideration	Product-based	Process-based
Is the aim to drive costs down as low as possible – are customers not sensitive to price?	Greater potential for cost reductions via technology, equipment and standardisation	More personalised service Generally more expensive
Is it important that every customer receives exactly the same service?	Offers greatest opportunity for standardisation and therefore consistency of service	Assumes that service needs to be personalised to the needs of individual customers
Is the service likely to change or need to be adapted at some stage in the future?	Offers limited flexibility – particularly when the service offering changes significantly	More flexibility to add or adapt service
What level of expertise or specialised skills are required to provide the service?	Appropriate when low levels of expertise are demanded	Suitable in services that require specialised sets of skills

number of rooms in a hotel, the number of vans owned by a delivery company, the number of seats in an aeroplane and so on is limited. Demand for services, conversely, is variable. Service capacity is the measure and management of how many customers a business can serve at the same time.

The first step is to work out what your capacity is, and the best way to achieve this is to draw a chart. Depending on your business you may want to use a scale that is expressed in hours, days, weeks or months.

Figure 7.3 is an example of a chart of demand and capacity for a restaurant (which is charted in hours). Notice how demand is low before 7 pm, rising to a peak around 7.30 pm, then falls back off after 9 pm. The maximum capacity of the business is determined by the number of people it can seat at any one time. There is also an optimum capacity utilisation line. First, however, let us consider situations (a), (b) and (c) as presented in the diagram.

At point (a) in the diagram, demand exceeds maximum capacity at peak hour – there are more people wanting a seat at the restaurant than there are available

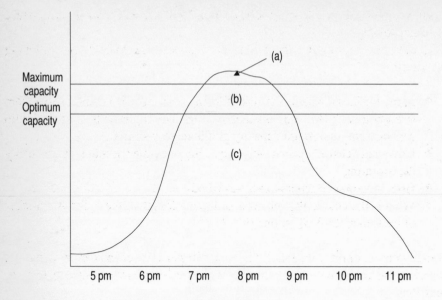

Figure 7.3 An example of demand and capacity

places. By implication, business is either *actually* lost (customers go elsewhere) or *potentially* lost (customers may be persuaded to come back later in the evening). Note, however, that for the majority of the evening, demand is nowhere near this capacity level, meaning that *fixed* resources are wasted.

At point (b) in the diagram, demand exceeds optimum capacity. This means that the customers can find seats at the restaurant; however, at this level of demand, there is serious risk of service quality declining. The busier the restaurant, the higher the risk of mistakes being made; service delays; customers getting frustrated by others around them; waiting and kitchen staff becoming flustered because of the pressure placed on them. The net result is that, while custom is not lost *on this occasion*, the risk of turning customers away in the future, due to an inferior service experience, increases.

At point (c) in the diagram, capacity exceeds demand – so much so, at times, that capacity is wasted. In these situations, the restaurant is losing money – paying for fixed and variable resources without servicing customers.

So what do we learn from this diagram?

First, we learn that the business that aims to match demand with maximum capacity suffers the risk of disappointing customers – and losing their custom in the long term. Consequently, we learn that an '*optimum capacity utilisation level*' – which is less than our maximum capacity – is likely to be a better goal for a service organisation, allowing it to deliver high levels of service to ensure customer loyalty.

To determine optimum capacity in your business ask yourself the following questions:

- In my business, what is the risk of losing customers if I cannot serve them straight away? (In some businesses, this risk might be low, so optimum capacity and maximum capacity could be very similar.)
- How many customers can we serve at any one time without service quality deteriorating?
- How long do customers expect to wait?
- What is the cost to my business of having less than the optimum number of customers through at one time?

In many cases, optimum capacity is about 80 per cent of maximum capacity; however, this figure will vary considerably, depending on your answers to these questions.

Once you have established what your optimum capacity is (in a restaurant it might be having two spare tables at any one time; in a plumbing business it might mean booking out only 80 per cent of your time in jobs for one day), the next step is to deal with the hard question of what to do when demand exceeds optimum capacity.

Think about a doctor's surgery with three full-time doctors and one receptionist. Here, the optimum capacity would be where all three doctors are seeing patients, with one patient in the waiting room. This level of capacity allows for emergencies to be dealt with quickly, the reception to be reasonably free, yet each doctor's time is not wasted waiting for patients to arrive.

Now consider demand for this type of service. Demand will typically exceed capacity at the following times:

- early morning (before work/school begins);
- lunch hour (assuming it is in a business district);
- late afternoon (after work/school);
- winter – when colds and flu are most prevalent;
- government warnings or media information aimed at preventive approaches to health.

Consider each of these. The first four causes are predictable and regular. These require a different strategy from those that are unpredictable.

Predictable and regular surges in demand

Where causes are predictable and regular, it will be difficult to dampen these surges in demand. There is little use offering patients incentives to get their cold and flu injections during summer, for instance, when they are not sick during that time. However, you are not powerless; strategies for managing demand peaks that are **predictable** and **regular** include:

- Manage *variable* capacity around these peaks and troughs. In the above example, the business might want to employ a nurse, part-time medico or extra receptionist just at these peak hours, and an additional full-time doctor during the winter months.
- Consider turning *fixed* capacity into variable capacity during peak season. This could be achieved by buying foldaway chairs and additional magazines during winter months or converting unused areas of the building into additional consultation rooms.
- Actively encourage demand in low periods. While difficult in a medical practice, it is still not impossible to move demand. Consider the role of the receptionist, for instance – he or she has the opportunity to manipulate demand for both phone-up and walk-in consultations. This opportunity should be used as much as possible.
- Communication, too, can readily encourage patients to come at different times, assuming their condition is not urgent. Price can be used to encourage demand away from peak hours (eg by imposing a peak-hour consultation fee, if feasible), as can highlighting other benefits (eg less than a five-minute wait guaranteed for appointments between 10 am and 11.30 am).

Unpredictable surges in demand

Not all demand fluctuations are predictable, however. These can cause distress for service businesses, so you need to develop rules that allow customers to be prioritised. In some cases, this might be the 'first in, first served' rule; in others, such as our doctor's surgery, patients are more likely to be prioritised according to the urgency of their condition. In either case, customers will typically have to wait for the service to be performed. Where waiting is evident, there are two key options to explore: a 'queuing system' and finding ways to 'reduce perceived waiting time'.

Queuing system

There are a number of different queuing systems available to service businesses. These include:

- 'one-to-one' system – where a single queue forms in front of a single operator (eg supermarket checkout);
- 'one-to-many' system – where a single queue forms and it then disperses to multiple operators (eg bank tellers);
- 'snake' system – where a single queue is formed and 'snakes' around to avoid a long straight line forming (eg airport customs);
- 'take-a-number' system – where customers take a number that dictates their place in 'line' (eg supermarket delicatessen).

Each queuing system has its advantages and disadvantages. The main issues to consider when determining the appropriate queuing design for your business are:

- How much room is available for queuing? (Is it feasible to have a single queue?)
- How long are customers likely to wait? (Will standing be an issue – that is, will you need to seat them?)
- How many operators do you have relative to the number of customers waiting at any one time?
- How 'fair' is the queuing system in the eyes of customers?
- Which queuing system has the shortest *perceived* wait?

Answering these questions can provide some interesting answers. In the United States, for instance, a single product-oriented queue used at one fast food chain was seen to be more satisfactory by customers than the multiple queues employed by another, even though waiting time was longer.

Knowing how your queuing system affects customers is important. Use your research skills learnt in Chapter 2. Get out there and become part of the queue. Talk to customers. Find out what they see as the best queuing system for your business.

Reduce perceived waiting time

We wait in lines every day. We wait behind someone at the ATM. We wait to have our goods scanned at the supermarket checkout. We wait on the phone to talk to a customer service representative. Even though we are used to waiting. . . we hate it. Waiting is frustrating because we have so many other things to do in our lives.

As a business, you know that customers hate waiting. To try to overcome this, you are probably trying to design your service so they don't wait, but this is not always possible. So what can you do?

The key insight into what can be done comes from studies conducted on perceived waiting times. Katz, Larson and Larson conducted a recent study on waiting times in a bank environment, and found that most customers overestimate their waiting time. Not only this, while most overestimates are around 25 per cent, many customers overestimate the waiting time by 100 per cent. More importantly, as *perceptions* of waiting time increase (independent of actual waiting time), customer dissatisfaction increases.

So, if you can change your customers' *perceptions* about waiting time, then you can minimise the degree to which the wait impacts upon customer dissatisfaction. To this end, there are eight rules to understanding and manipulating perceptions of waiting time:

- Unoccupied time feels longer than occupied time.
- Pre-process waits feel longer than in-process waits.
- Anxiety makes waits seem even longer.
- Uncertain waits seem longer than known, finite waits.
- Unexplained waits appear longer than explained waits.
- Unfair waits feel longer than equitable waits.
- Waiting for a valuable service (from the customer's point of view) seems shorter.
- Solo waiting feels longer than group waiting.

So what can you do to minimise perceived wait time? Here are some ideas:

- Entertain and distract. Install distractions that keep your customer physically involved. Music might provide a nice atmosphere, but is probably insufficient to keep them sufficiently occupied to influence their perception of waiting time. Many businesses now install mirrors near elevators; doctors' surgeries have televisions as well as magazines; banks sometimes employ electronic news bulletins. One dental surgeon even has a menu of videos for patients to choose from while waiting, with a television monitor hanging from the ceiling for them to enjoy their selected show during oral surgery.
- Get customers out of line and/or into the process. Provide alternatives (ie telephone and Internet banking) that get customers out of queues; involve them in the process. For example, Sydney airport customs employed officials to check the documentation and passports of incoming passengers while they were in the queue during the Sydney Olympic period. This avoided delays at the customs counter and made customers feel part of the process while they were still in the queuing stages.

- Inform customers about waits. If you know how long they will be waiting, tell them. If there is a reason for longer than usual waits, customers need to know *why*.
- Keep non-active resources out of site. There is nothing more frustrating for the bank customer in a queue than seeing tellers chatting and talking on the phone behind the teller's desk.
- Segment customers according to their willingness to wait. Express-lane checkouts at supermarkets have been developed for these reasons.
- Never underestimate the power of a friendly server to appease the sense of waiting and provide a strong recovery effort.

The role of physical products

Evan was running late. He was supposed to have met his mates at the rugby club over an hour ago. He had finally broken free from the traffic jam and would be there in a few minutes, but he had to get some cash before he arrived.

He pulled up in front of the bank and rushed up to the ATM. He hadn't used this kind of machine before, but then again, he hadn't ever really taken much notice of any of the machines.

He pushed his plastic card through the slot and began to tap his fingers impatiently. The machine made some noise, and then spat the card out, signalling an 'error' message. Frustrated, Evan reinserted the card – only to achieve the same result. He removed the card, rubbed it against his jeans, and tried again. This time the machine simply swallowed his card and the message on the screen told him that he would have to contact the bank during business hours to retrieve it.

Not only was Evan even later still – now he would have to show up without money.

Had Evan not been in such a rush, he would have noticed a sign on the new ATM showing him that he was putting his card in the wrong way round. While this was probably a more functional *technical* ATM, the design technicians had overlooked an important fact: that humans are creatures of habit. We learn to put our plastic card in a certain way, we get used to driving on the same side of the road, we like to know where the butter is at the local supermarket. Challenging these mental patterns can be confusing and frustrating, and demands effective signage and the 'retraining' of customer behaviour.

When designing services, or service components, we need to remember that physical products play three roles:

- a **functional** role – so a shopping trolley is designed to make it as easy as possible for the customer to wheel around the supermarket and load their shopping (apparently it is not designed to have a mind of its own);
- an **aesthetic** role – so wooden interiors, leather furniture and dimmed lighting might be used to create atmosphere in a bar;
- a **symbolic** role – so red lights are used to signal closed lanes or areas in a car park, whereas green arrows indicate the 'right' direction or parking areas.

Think about your business for a moment and make a list of the types of physical products that your customers enjoy. Then complete Table 7.3 by putting a tick or cross in each column depending on your approach, using the definitions below.

Table 7.3 Analysing your physical products

Product	Two-way model used	Visibility mapping	Consistent	Feedback	Affordance	Constraints	Control

This list has been constructed on the basis of studies of human relationships with everyday products. Your completed table will provide you with insights into how the customer aspects of your physical products could be improved.

'Two-way' models

Typically, a service is designed, and then customers are forced to interact with that service. Too rarely do we see information flowing in the reverse direction, with customers sharing their experiences and providing the service designers with feedback or ideas. Sure, many of the major design faults will be picked up in customer complaints over time, but once the service is up and running, often these faults are difficult and expensive to change.

Feedback in the design stages is therefore critical. Ask your customers what they think of your new product before you introduce it. Find out whether there are any usage problems. Do you need clearer signage or explanations? Ask a number of customers – and be sure to include customers of all ages, backgrounds and major disabilities.

Visibility

It is one thing to have clear instructions on how to use your product but if no one notices the instructions, the service design has failed. It is often better to assume that customers know nothing. Some classic examples include lighting in hotel rooms, taps in bathrooms and how to use a telephone. These may be simple things to most of us in our own country, but think of your first experience in another country – it was probably frustrating because the familiar had become new, and your expectations do not apply in these circumstances. For example, consider the door handles in Finland. There the handle not only serves to open the door, but is also used for locking doors when the handle is turned in the opposite direction. While this might be self-explanatory to a Finn, foreign visitors might have an embarrassing experience before they learn this trick.

Create consistent mapping

People learn through associating causes and effects. Take Evan's ATM experience, for instance – a frustrating one created by changing the 'rules' of behaviour. This does not mean you should avoid innovation in service design. What it does mean, however, is that you need to realise that customers have expectations built up through years of service interactions. If you have a strong reason to want to change this behaviour, remember to tell your customers this clearly in order to avoid frustration and confusion. Also, make sure that you use the same sets of 'rules' wherever possible (for example, go right for the fast queue). Customers will be much happier and there will be fewer service 'hiccups' if you work *with* current behaviour rather than trying to change it.

Provide feedback

Often customers are uncertain about how to use a machine or service component – particularly if they are a first-time user. Think about the first time you went to use the hydraulic weights at the gym, or you first encountered telephone banking.

To help reduce customer uncertainty and to reinforce correct usage, provide confirmation cues. Imagine, for instance, you were trying to call someone on your mobile phone. Wouldn't it be frustrating not to hear any sound after you had dialled the number? Instead of hearing silence, telecommunications companies use different tones as a form of feedback – to let the customer know what is happening with their call. The same is true of many Internet transactions, with confirmation responses being sent to the customers' e-mail addresses. Even if your service doesn't require complex technology, think about how you can provide appropriate feedback so that customers' cognitive control is increased.

Affordance

The term 'affordance' refers to the real and perceived qualities of a product that need to be recognised before they are integrated into the service design. A single product might have a number of uses. Take the hotel room chair, for instance. While the chair might be intended for the hotel guest to sit on, that same guest might choose to hang his or her clothes on it, or stand on it to reach high places. If the chair is not designed with these other uses in mind, it may not perform under each of these conditions.

Constraints

Constraints should be used when you want to avoid misuse of a particular service component. For example, bright orange cones or other types of traffic constraints are used when roads are under repair to make sure motorists take the appropriate detour.

We can sometimes take constraint 'tools' from signals we have become familiar with – like traffic lights. If green means 'go' in a particular culture, then it is not a particularly useful colour if we want to stop customers going somewhere.

A supermarket recently had trouble with congestion in the middle of shopping aisles. The simple act of painting a white line down the centre of the supermarket aisles provided sufficient learnt cues (road rules) to alleviate this problem. Shoppers moving down the aisle stuck to the left-hand side of the white line, while those coming the other way stayed on the other side.

Control possibilities for customers

The flight had been delayed, the cab driver was rude and the change in climate was an unpleasant shock. Jacqui was happy to have finally arrived at the hotel. The hotel room was nice enough, but it was stuffy and smelt a little musty. Throwing her bag down on the bed, she went over to open the window. It was sealed shut. Frustrated, Jacqui had to settle for turning up the air-conditioning in her room. An hour later, the room was too cold, but the musty smell lingered.

In Chapter 1, we talked about the notion of customer control. Part of this was the idea of decisional control, or giving customers choices. If, in this instance, Jacqui had had a choice of being able to open the window, it is likely that she would have been a happy hotel guest. As it was, the lack of choice was frustrating as it left her feeling unable to control the conditions of her room.

Process improvement

Services are made up from a number of different processes. Just something simple like buying a coffee and a croissant in the morning is supported by a string of activities. First, there is the process of producing and providing the menu; there is the ordering process, the delivery of the goods, and the payment process. The performance of each of these elements has an impact on the customers' perception of the overall quality of service. It has an impact that goes beyond that day, and forms their opinion about whether or not they should come back.

Generally, when customers decide not to come back to a service, it is because the service they have received has failed to meet their expectations on at least one of the service process components. Do you have a problem with your service processes? One way to find out is to diagnose your processes using the 'Gaps Model' (Figure 7.4).

The Gaps Model was designed by academics studying service quality. The idea is that every service process begins with a set of expectations that is created by listening to what others say about that service (word of mouth), by an individual customer's personal needs and by his or her past experience with that particular service.

Take the example of Becky ordering a coffee and croissant, for instance. Becky might visit the cafeteria because it was recommended by her work colleagues (word of mouth). On this particular morning, she might be running late for work, so she is in a hurry (personal needs). She has been to this café once before and received polite, efficient and accurate service (past experience). What does she therefore expect? She expects to be served exactly what she orders very quickly and politely.

On this particular occasion, the woman serving Becky recognised her from the week before and stopped work to have a friendly chat. This slowed things down. Concentrating on having her friendly chat, the woman serving her forgot that Becky wanted jam on her croissant, so Becky didn't get the meal she wanted. She ended up leaving the café frustrated and late for her morning meeting.

Sounds like a pretty simple example of how service processes could go wrong. According to the Gaps Model, there are four key gaps that can contribute to the fifth and most critical gap: the failure of the service delivered to meet the customer's expectations:

Conceptual Model of Service Quality

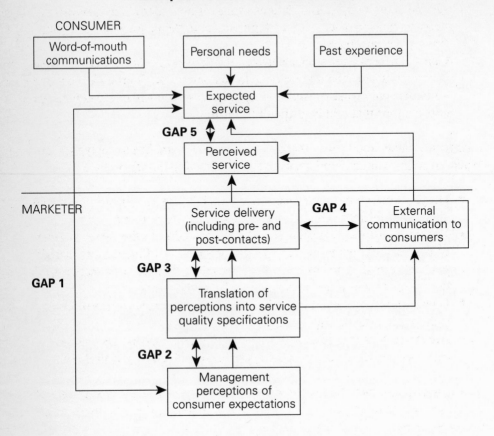

Figure 7.4 The 'Gaps Model'. Adapted from V Zeithaml, L L Berry and A Parasuraman, Communication and control processes in the delivery of service quality, *Journal of Marketing*, **52** (April 1988), pp 35–48

Gap 1: There is a difference between customer expectations and management's perceptions of these expectations. In this instance, management thought the customer wanted a friendly, polite chat. Instead, she was in a hurry and wanted fast, efficient service.

Gap 2: There is a difference between management perceptions of consumer expectations and service delivery specifications. Even if management recognised the need for fast efficient service, are the systems and processes set up so that this can be delivered?

Gap 3: There is a difference between service quality specifications and the service actually delivered. It doesn't matter how many rules and procedures you have in place – if you don't deliver to them, you will not be satisfying your customers.

Gap 4: There is a difference between the delivery of the service and what is communicated about the service to customers. Don't promise the world – promise only what you can deliver; otherwise you will create heightened expectations that will be difficult to fulfil.

Having now understood where these gaps arise, you might like to apply the Gaps Model in your business. Find answers to the following questions:

- Do you know what your customers expect? Is what you communicate about your business creating the right set of expectations?
- Different customers expect different things and even the same customer can expect different things (eg speed of service) on different occasions. Do you and your staff understand what drives these different expectations and how to spot them when a customer walks in the door?
- Is your knowledge about what customers like effectively translated into the right service standards?
- Are the service standards achievable? Are they understood and respected by your staff? Are the staff empowered and enabled to deliver them?

Now that you have identified some of the problem areas or 'gaps' in your service processes, you will be ready to *close the gap*. Closing the gap involves the following steps:

1. Identify the problem.
2. Understand the cause.
3. Implement problem solution.
4. Communicate problem solution initiative.
5. Measure the effect of service process change on customers.

So, in this chapter we have seen how to design the workings of your business so that customers are given the consideration that they deserve. The next challenge is to locate your business in the place where the greatest number of customers can find it. This is covered in the next chapter.

8 *Location, location, location*

Two dry-cleaning businesses operate in the local area. One opens onto a noisy main thoroughfare and the other is a couple of streets away, positioned between a newsagent and a beauty salon in a busy, but quiet side street.

Which of these two businesses do you think is the more profitable, assuming that overheads and service levels are similar in each?

Location is part of your service package, and for many businesses the choice of location is the key to success. Consider your own business for a moment. What problems have you experienced with the location you have chosen? How does it affect your level of business? Does it cut you away from certain kinds of customers? Does it satisfy the emotional needs of those customers you want to do business with? Is it plainly inconvenient?

If you have done everything suggested in this book and you are still not enjoying success then it is likely that your location is holding you back, and you should be actively looking for ways to make a change – fast.

Finding the right location involves more than simply looking at the price (whether buying, developing or leasing). When choosing a location you need to consider the following elements:

- context;
- economics;
- demography;
- site attributes;
- geographic representation.

Context

There are three aspects of context:

- the nature of the service;
- access;
- competition.

The nature of the service

The service context will dictate what is important both to customers and to you. For some services (such as those offered by outdoor cafés or hotel resorts), the natural beauty of the surroundings will be strong draw-cards. For others (such as plumbing services or medical facilities), expensive premises in nice surroundings are an unnecessary expense.

Access

Think about how customers access your service – is it something they will travel out of their way for (eg a special sporting facility), or is business likely to be driven by convenience (eg a service station or convenience store)? Is parking likely to be important to customers, to staff or to suppliers? Are there any specific materials that you should be located close to, or any supply considerations/risks that you need to consider?

Competition

Think, too, about the immediate competitive environment. How close or distant is your service from its competitors? One common fallacy is that you should distance yourself as far as possible from your competitors. This is not always true. Think of the 'Auto Alleys' and Supercentres. This 'nesting' of competing firms in the same area creates a 'zone of expertise' that will attract customers to that area.

Economics

When looking at the cost of a location (whether purchasing, developing or leasing), be sure to look deeper than simply the face value of the property or site you are after. Important considerations include:

- demand growth/flexibility considerations;
- costs or limitations of site modification;
- future potential or limitations of the location;
- positive or adverse environment or extraneous effects (pollution, corrosion);
- cost of security and insurance.

Demography

The demography of the local population is an important consideration for service organisations. In some cases, the emphasis will be business customers; in others it will be individual customers or customer households. The successful service enterprise must be close to, or at least accessible to, its target customer base.

Site attributes

As a starting point, here are some site attributes to consider:

- health and safety;
- local and government zoning (including future development);
- legal and licensing considerations;
- traffic flows;
- people counts (the number of pedestrians passing a given point in a set time).

Some sites will be adversely affected by climate; others limited by availability of local resources. In other situations, town planning or local government regulations might affect the ability of a service business to operate profitably in that area.

You need to think through all the variables to be able to choose the best site for your business. However, remember that as your business develops over time, the site that was perfect at the beginning may no longer serve you now. You need to review regularly how your choice of location supports your business to make sure that what started as an asset has not become a liability.

One of the ways to work through the site selection question is to complete the worksheet provided in Table 8.1. The best way to use this sheet is to think about the service you are offering and imagine that you are going through the process of selecting a new location or site for your business.

Table 8.1 Location analysis ✗

Consideration	Importance	Site A rating	Site A total	Site B rating	Site B total
Easy to see and find the business					
Business is easy to get to					
Easy to park					
Attractive location/environment					
Local population fits target market					
Growth potential					
Flexibility to modify or expand business					
Cost of acquisition and modifications					
Legal and safety considerations					
Climatic conditions relevant to service ⌐					
Proximity to competitors					
Proximity to suppliers					
Cost of security and insurance					
Traffic flows/passer-by traffic					
Image fits with organisation & culture					
TOTALS					

Importance column

To begin with, work through the following list of considerations and rate each in terms of its importance to your business performance. Some considerations might be important because of the effect they have on attracting customers; others might be important because of the potential risk they pose to the stability or performance of the business. Either way, give each consideration a score from 0 to 10 where '10' means 'Critical' and 1 means 'Not important at all'. Give any consideration a '0' if you feel it is not applicable to your industry or business.

Note: In the real world, different services would choose a different set of considerations, depending on what attributes they consider to be critical success factors.

Site A and Site B ratings

Now think of two potential sites for your new business. Feel free to consider more than two sites by simply extending the number of columns in the table. You can call these potential locations Site A and Site B, respectively. Now go through the list of considerations that you have just rated. For any consideration that has not rated a '0' in the importance column (ie will have some impact on the likely success of the business), rate each site in terms of how well it fulfils each consideration. Again, use a scale from 1 to 10, where '10' is 'Excellent' and '1' is 'Poor'. It doesn't matter what the points in between are, as long as you use the scale consistently across the sites you are rating. Note: When you come to 'proximity to competitors', remember that it is better to be closer to your competitors than further from them.

Calculating site totals

The site evaluation totals will be a combination of how important each consideration is and the score given to each site for that factor. In other words, for each line in the table, multiply your figure from the Importance column and the figure from the Site A rating column to generate a figure for the Site A total column. Repeat the same procedure for Site B and any other sites you are interested in rating.

Adding the site totals

The final step is to add the site total columns at the bottom of the table. These totals can now be directly compared against one another to help select the best site available for your business. The bigger the score, the better the site will be – not only accounting for the relevant site attributes, but taking into account how important each of these attributes is to the overall success of your business.

This tool is obviously critical to managers starting a business from scratch or selecting a new location. It is also useful, however, to existing businesses to help identify location-related sources of competitive advantage or disadvantage. Consider completing the above template again – this time comparing your business with that of a prominent competitor. How much does locational advantage or disadvantage contribute to performance in your industry? Identify areas of weakness in the table you have just completed. Now, go through each in turn and rate them in terms of your ability to do something to overcome these weaknesses. Give those easiest to overcome an 'A' rating; those most difficult to address a 'C' rating, and all in between a 'B' rating.

Review the list of 'A' rating attributes. Can your organisation develop an action plan that might help overcome some of these weaknesses in the immediate or medium-term future?

Geographic representation

Now that you have identified some key elements, it is time to ask a more difficult set of questions.

An ice-cream vendor opens up for business on a beach. Where is the ideal place for the vendor to locate his or her ice-cream stall?

The answer to this question might seem simple – why, the vendor should locate in the middle of the beach so he or she maximises the chance of gaining traffic from both ends of the beach (assuming even distribution of bathers along the beach).

A second ice-cream vendor opens up his or her business on the same beach. Where is the ideal place for the new vendor to locate his or her ice-cream stall?

As mentioned in this chapter, the theory of competition tells you that the ideal place for the second vendor is directly adjacent to the first vendor. Here, you will automatically capture some of the initial vendor's market (second-mover advantage) – fishing, if you like, where the fish are.

Now, what happens if you are the twenty-first ice-cream vendor to open up a business on the same beach? What happens if you are selling to a group of customers who are scattered all around the town, and the best place to put your business is not obvious?

If you are faced with these situations, then you need to apply a mathematical model to reveal the best place for your business. There are several different types of models that you could use, including:

- the metropolitan metric;
- the Euclidean metric;
- the gravity model.

These can become pretty complicated, and in this chapter we describe how to apply the metropolitan metric (which is the one you are most likely to use) and overview the other two models.

Metropolitan metric

This method assumes that the only way that someone can get from A to B is to move in a 'grid' pattern – ie up and across or down and across. Imagine a street map, for instance, where all the streets run completely parallel or perpendicular to one another. The arrows show the only way a person can travel, on foot or by vehicle, from point A to destination B.

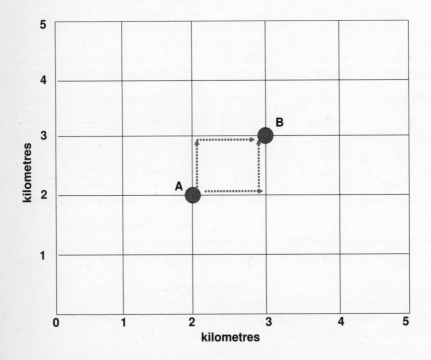

Figure 8.1 An example of a map of a town centre

Now, imagine that the streets were measured on the grid in miles so that there are measures along the horizontal or *x* axis as well as along the vertical or *y* axis. On this grid, imagine that you then identify four critical 'pockets' of consumers. To bring this to light, you can use the following example:

Starch 'n' Spark are a dry-cleaning service. Starch 'n' Spark want help identifying where they should locate their service in a town with four large apartment buildings. Apartment building 1 has 700 residents; apartment building 2 has 100 residents; apartment building 3 has 300 residents; and apartment building 4 has 500 residents. The location of each of the four apartment buildings is shown in Figure 8.2.

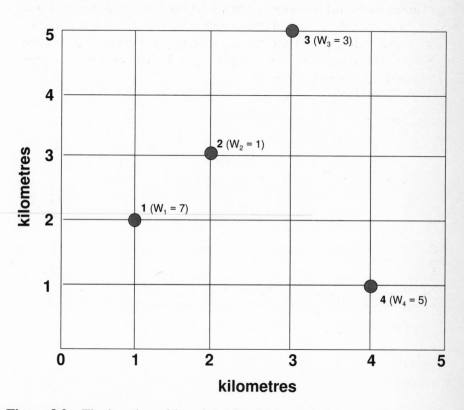

Figure 8.2 The location of Starch 'n' Spark's potential customers

The number of people in each apartment is translated into a weighting factor, represented next to the location of each building.

Now, the metropolitan metric approach tells you that the **best** location for Starch 'n' Spark is where the weighted distance travelled by its customers (or potential customers) is minimised. Because you know that customers must travel along a grid system, the calculation for this is quite simple: all you need to do is follow five steps.

Step 1 – Calculate the median weight of all of the 'pockets' of customers

To calculate a median, all you do is add up the weights of each of the pockets of customers and divide this total by 2. In this case, therefore, your calculation is as follows:

$(7 + 1 + 3 + 5) \div 2$
$= 16 \div 2$
$= 8$

Step 2 – Moving from left to right across the grid, total the weights of each demand point until you reach or exceed the median value

Start at the very left side of the grid. Now move your eyes (or follow with your finger) across the map towards your right. As you come across a demand point, note down the weight associated with this point. As you come across the next demand point, moving from left to right, add this weight to the one you have already written down. When you reach or exceed the median value you calculated above, stop and draw a *vertical dotted line* through that demand point.

In this example, the first point you come across is apartment building 1. The weight associated with this building is 7, so this is the first number. The second point you come across is building 2. This has a demand weight of 1. Adding 7 and 1 gives us 8, which is exactly equal to the median value you calculated earlier. Consequently, you can stop and draw your vertical dotted line through this demand point (or apartment building 2).

Step 3 – Now repeat this process, this time moving from right to left across the grid

Start at the right side of the grid and work your way across to the left-hand side. This time, you will come across apartment building 4 first. The weight here is 5. Next, you will come across apartment building 3; the weight here is 3. Because 5 and 3 total the median value of 8, you can stop and draw a vertical line through demand point 3 (or apartment building 3).

Step 4 – Follow exactly the same process (steps 2 and 3) to determine the best y coordinate

This time, start at the top of the grid and work your way down. You follow exactly the same process, except this time you will draw a *horizontal* line through the appropriate demand point. In this example, moving from top to bottom, the first point you reach is apartment building 3 with a weight of 3. The next is apartment building 2, with a weight of 1. Since 3 and 1 only total 4 (you need to reach or exceed 8), you keep moving down the grid. The next point is apartment building 1, with a weight of 7. Adding this to your sub-total of 4 puts you over the median target of 8, so you can stop and draw a horizontal line through the point where apartment 1 is located.

Now, moving from south to north (or bottom to top), follow the same process. This time, coincidentally, you stop at the location of apartment 1, so the horizontal line you draw is in exactly the same place as the one you have just drawn (you don't need to draw the line twice).

Step 5 – Identify the 'ideal zone' for the business location
The ideal zone will be the vertical and horizontal lines you have just drawn. In this case, because your horizontal limits were in the same place, the solution is a simple one: you should locate Starch 'n' Spark on your horizontal line between the two vertical lines as shown in Figure 8.3.

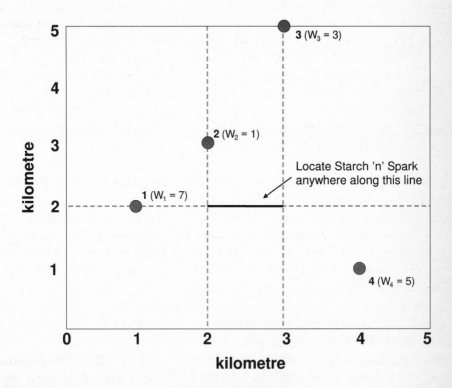

Figure 8.3   The best place to locate Starch 'n' Spark

This may be a lot more maths than you have previously applied when choosing a site, but these straightforward steps have transformed a critical decision from a best guess to a best possible outcome.

Other models

The metropolitan metric is great when you have a grid system, and works for many different kinds of businesses. However, some services cannot be calculated in this way. Take the example of a rural veterinary clinic where the vet can simply get on his or her motorbike and travel cross-country to the injured animal, or Federal Express's selection of Memphis as its only hub of air package delivery network to service the entire United States.

In these cases – where the most likely way to get from A to B is by taking a direct path – you need to use a different approach based on slightly different mathematical principles. This approach is called the 'Euclidean metric' approach and involves a considerably more complex and reiterative process than the metropolitan metric. For this reason, we will not run through the mathematics here, but if you want more information please e-mail the authors on www.lakegroup.com.au.

Another great tool is the gravity model, which is used by retailers to estimate the attractiveness of any given site. This model is based on principles of physics, and calculates the degree to which a facility is attractive to a customer based on:

- the size of the facility;
- the travel time from the customer's location to the facility;
- an estimate of the importance of travel time that accounts for the type of service you are considering (eg a department store vs a convenience store).

The model is quite complex, but if you know how much the average customers from different areas spend at your type of store (fruit and vegetable), you can use this information to calculate the likely revenue and market share under different site location conditions. Again, send us an e-mail if you have a particular interest in this model.

So, in this chapter you have teased out the key issues that you should consider when choosing a site. If you are already operating from a location, you should review your current position using these principles. If you are in the wrong spot, do all you can to move to a better place – as soon as possible.

9 Measuring your performance

Holly wasn't happy.

She had taken the morning off work to wait for the repair person – again. She had been given the 'He is on his way' runaround for the past hour.

There was no way that she would ever buy that product again – or any product in the range. There was nothing on earth that would make her recommend that service provider to any of her friends.

She would have her revenge.

This chapter shows you how to measure both customer satisfaction and your levels of service performance. It concludes with an example that shows how to use measures to improve your performance. This chapter is for the hundreds like Holly who are waiting at home right now – the victims of poor service standards and blunt satisfaction measures.

Measuring customer satisfaction

Home loan customer

'The home loans officer we spoke to was terrific – I was quite nervous about everything, being my first home and all, but she just made everything seem so simple and easy. She was lovely.'

Airline customer

'The flight – yeah, it was fine. The plane took off when it was supposed to; there were no problems along the way – the plane arrived safely. . . it was fine.'

Customer buying sports shoes

'The guy just wanted to make a sale – he gave me the typical sales spiel and didn't really give a damn about what I wanted. I think he must have been paid on commission or something, he was just trying to push me into buying. He didn't listen to me – I just got frustrated in the end and left without buying anything.'

Catering customer

'I asked them to cater for my wife's fortieth birthday. I had no idea at all what I wanted, but they were terrific: they suggested the menu, ran through all the details with me, then, on the day, they were smart, professional, the food was awesome and everyone commented what a fantastic job I'd done organising everything. What's more, they left the place looking like it had just been spring-cleaned. Absolutely fantastic – would recommend them to anyone and will definitely be using them if I need catering again in the future.'

These statements from customers provide valuable insights into the customer's experience. In the case of the airline customer, the service has clearly met a very basic level of expectation, so the customer could be described as 'satisfied'. This is very different, however, from the catering customer, who is clearly delighted with his experience.

So what is customer satisfaction all about, and what do you need to do to make sure that you understand and deliver the right level of satisfaction for your business? To measure customer satisfaction you need to do the following:

- Identify what should be measured.
- Understand customer expectations.
- Identify your customers' zones of tolerance.
- Develop measures that show how you are performing.

Identify what should be measured

Customer satisfaction is not driven by everything that your organisation does. It is delivered by getting a small number of key events/interactions/moments right. These are what Jan Carlzon called the 'moments of truth' – they have a disproportionate effect on the way in which customers view their whole experience with your business. You need to attach customer satisfaction measures to these moments.

There are probably between five and eight key moments of truth for your organisation. They are reasonably obvious, and while customers may not be able to articulate them immediately, you will find them through a combination of observation, interviews and focus groups (see Chapter 2).

You do not need to use all these techniques extensively, and you will probably get most of the information that you need simply by sitting/walking next to a customer as he or she progresses through the full range of experiences with your organisation. You need to note where the moments of truth occur, and what happened. You can then supplement this information through a small number of interviews and focus groups. You should ask three questions:

- If you get nothing else right, what is the one thing that you would hope was properly attended to?
- When you make a judgement about what kind of business we are, what information do you use?
- Can you give me an example of one situation that was particularly memorable the last time you did business with us?

The result of this research will be a list of the key moments that you need to track and measure actively.

Once you have this list of the key service interactions it is tempting to go directly to developing one of those little 'customer satisfaction' surveys that you probably get every time you stay in a hotel. This would be a mistake, not because the questionnaire would be flawed (you will build one a little later in this chapter), but because you will not know what to do with the answers. To interpret the results properly you need to know about customer expectations and their zone of tolerance.

Understand customer expectations

Customer expectations are important, because satisfying customers is all about meeting or exceeding their expectations.

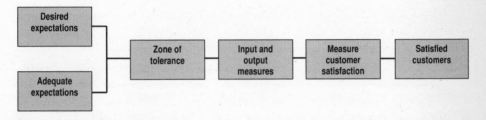

Figure 9.1   The customer satisfaction sequence

There are two parts to understanding customer expectations: 'identifying desired and adequate expectations' and 'identifying the customer's zone of tolerance'.

Identifying desired and adequate expectations

Customers have two levels of expectations. At the higher end of the scale, customers have 'desired service expectations'. At the other end there are 'adequate service expectations'.

Desired service expectations

Desired service expectations are, to a large extent, expectations that few organisations can afford to meet. They are developed through:

- Personal needs at a particular point in time. For instance, a customer visiting the hairdresser might be in a hurry one day, so the speed of service becomes an important expectation. On another occasion, the same customer might have a strong need to be pampered or fussed over. Both are desired service expectations, even though they are different.
- Expectations of others. A customer booking a holiday through a travel agent might be doing so on behalf of others (partner or family). Consequently, the needs, wants and desires of the others he or she is representing will be integrated into that customer's desired service expectations, even though they may not represent the needs, wants or desires of that particular customer.
- Importance of the service experience. A customer taking important international clients to a restaurant will have a different set of expectations than if he or she were visiting the same restaurant with a colleague for a regular lunch or dinner. The importance of the situation will typically mean a higher level of desired service expectations irrespective of the wants and needs of other parties involved in the service.

Take a few minutes and note down five expectations that five of your customers have that fit into the category of 'desired service expectations.'

Adequate service expectations

Adequate service expectations are driven by a customer's past experience with that kind of service, and more particularly with that particular provider. However, it is not simply that you expect exactly what you got last time; customers are generous enough to factor in situational occurrences that are seen to be beyond the control of the service provider.

Table 9.1   Your examples of desired service expectations

Customer	Desired service expectation 1	Desired service expectation 2	Desired service expectation 3	Desired service expectation 4	Desired service expectation 5
Customer 1					
Customer 2					
Customer 3					
Customer 4					
Customer 5					

Customers are realistic (well, most of the time). They recognise that what they want cannot always be delivered. A customer staying at a popular resort over Easter or Christmas knows that resources are stretched, so service levels may drop. Customers know that their accountant will be busy at financial year-end, and cannot always get them out of having to pay taxes (if you know one who can, please let us know). Similarly, an employment agency customer appreciates that his or her employment opportunities are constrained by factors beyond the control of the agency (skill set, economic climate, types of jobs available, and so on).

As before, note down five adequate service expectations that five of your customers have of your organisation.

Table 9.2   Your examples of adequate service expectations

Customer	Adequate service expectation 1	Adequate service expectation 2	Adequate service expectation 3	Adequate service expectation 4	Adequate service expectation 5
Customer 1					
Customer 2					
Customer 3					
Customer 4					
Customer 5					

Identify your customers' zone of tolerance

Between these two levels of expectations lies the 'zone of tolerance'. This is the area in which the service rendered is likely to satisfy, but not necessarily delight, the customer.

Figure 9.2   Basic zone of tolerance

Typically there are two zones, which are driven by two different factors.

There are technical factors – which are about the outcomes of the service. For a hairdressing customer, for instance, the technical outcome is the look and feel of the hairstyle they end up with. Generally, a customer's zone of tolerance will be both higher and smaller for technical factors. After all, there is little point in having your clothes dry-cleaned, for instance, if they are returned dirty.

There are also process factors – which relate to the manner in which the service is provided. For the same hairdressing customer the process outcomes include the timeliness and professionalism of the service, how clean the premises were, the quality of the docket he or she received, and so on. These factors are more determined by the situation and influenced by personal tastes, and so expectations will typically be lower and the zone of tolerance broader.

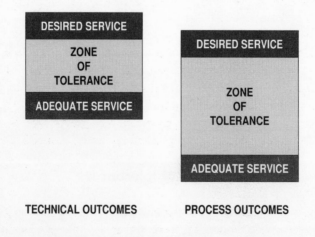

Figure 9.3   The two zones of tolerance

To develop a clear picture of the contents of the zones of tolerance, create a three-column table. You already have a list of the items that you need to measure, so insert this list into the first column. In the second column you are going to enter what customers see as adequate, and in the third you will enter what they categorise as desired service.

Table 9.3   Identifying your zone of tolerance

Items you need to measure	Adequate service	Desired service

You have already gained some insights when you guessed at the five examples of adequate and desired service levels for five customers. You can now use these to develop research and gather more precise information. This comes from three sources (see Chapters 2 and 6)

Internal research
Interviews and focus groups will make explicit what is in your customers' heads. Either talk them through, or physically walk them through, your key interactions. Ask them to describe what they would reasonably expect, and what would surprise and delight them. Note their responses.

Complaints
In Chapter 6 we talked about complaints being free research. This is an opportunity to plunder the complaints' data bank and withdraw all the information that you have about your key service interactions. Create two piles: those complaints that are about times when the customer has not received adequate levels of service, and those where they are disappointed because they failed to get desired levels of service. Note the level of performance that is implied by this information.

Your front line
The people on your front line probably have a good understanding of where the adequate and desired limits exist. Interviews and focus groups similar to those you have conducted with customers will produce the information you need.

Once you have these three pieces of information you can complete the table that you have been given so far (Table 9.3). However, you need to add two more columns, and two more pieces of information.

Table 9.4 Identifying the right level of satisfaction for your business

Items you need to measure	Adequate service	Desired service	Your zone of tolerance	Your desired position

Your zone of tolerance

You can now calculate and describe the zone of tolerance – and place this information in the fourth column. This is relatively straightforward, and captures the upper and lower levels of the zone in a clean, clear statement.

Your desired position

Few organisations can afford to provide a level of service that is at the upper end of the zone of tolerance on every key interaction. Most may be able to perform well in only one or two, and provide adequate levels for the rest. Go back to Chapter 3 and confirm your service strategy. It will dictate which part of this zone you need to occupy. The trick is to organise your business so that you deliver outcomes for customers that are within their zone of tolerance, but cost you no more than is absolutely necessary.

You now have the information that you need to produce a table similar to Table 9.5.

So, you now have the interactions that need to be measured, a zone of tolerance for each one, and a position that you want to occupy in each zone for strategic reasons. To test that this is happening, you need to measure your levels of customer satisfaction.

Develop measures that show how you are performing

Now that you know what you are looking for, you can start to track customer satisfaction. This is achieved as follows:

- Create measures that lead to action.
- Develop the questionnaire to collect the data.

Table 9.5 Example: A plumbing service (repair)

Item	Desired level	Adequate level	Zone of tolerance	Desired position
Speed of service	Available within 1 hour	Available within 48 hours	Available within 1–48 hrs	Urgent service (aim for 1-hour response time at premium price) Standard service (aim for service within 36 hrs)
Repair efficiency	100% rectification of problem	90% rectification of problem	90–100% rectification of problem	Aim for 95% rectification within time allocated Provide a separate quote for a bigger job
Cleanliness	Plumber leaves area in pristine condition	Plumber leaves area as it was on arrival	Leaving area as clean as found	Plumber cleans up mess directly related to the work completed

- Give the questionnaire to the right people.
- Analyse the results.

Create measures that lead to action

Jasmine looked at the customer satisfaction results. Customers were less satisfied this month than they had been for a long time, but she did not know why. She knew she could probably find out if she did some more research, but by that time the results might have corrected themselves anyway.

Jasmine decided she would just wait and see what happened with next quarter's results.

Managers like Jasmine find themselves trying to use data that are virtually meaningless because the measures have not been constructed in the right way. There are two types of measures that you need to design: 'output measures' and 'input/explanatory measures'.

Output measures

Output measures (also known as dependent variables) tell you how well you are performing. These output measures are used in conjunction with the information that you have about your zone of tolerance. They tell you about how well you are meeting your intention to occupy your chosen place in the zone, and whether or not your zone is still in the right place in your industry. The three most common measures are:

- absolute measures;
- expectation-based measures;
- competitor-based measures.

Absolute measures

Absolute measures relate to a satisfaction scale, without any references to any particular internal or external frames of reference. The kinds of questions are as follows:

Overall, how satisfied would you say you were with the service you received:

Very satisfied	☐
Satisfied	☐
Neither satisfied nor dissatisfied	☐
Dissatisfied	☐
Very dissatisfied	☐

Expectations measures

Expectation measures ask the customer to compare the service with their expectations. The style of questions is as follows:

Overall, would you say the service you received was:

A lot better than expected	☐
A little better than expected	☐
Much as expected	☐
A little worse than expected	☐
A lot worse than expected	☐

Competitor measures

These probe differences between your business and your competitors. The questions are as follows:

Overall, would you say the service you received was:

A lot better than for other businesses in this industry	☐
A little better than for other businesses in this industry	☐
Much the same as for other businesses in this industry	☐
A little worse than for other businesses in this industry	☐
A lot worse than for other businesses in this industry	☐

The examples provided here all relate to overall perceptions. You can also use these measures to examine specific items. Later in this chapter you will design a questionnaire using these kinds of questions. Essentially, any or all of these satisfaction measures can be used, depending on how long you wish to make the questionnaire. It does not matter too much which type of measure you use, as long as you a) keep using the same measure over time so you can identify change, and b) ensure you have *input* questions included as well, so you can *diagnose* the drivers of your current performance.

Input measures

Input measures (also known as independent variables) enable you to understand *why* customers are rating their satisfaction at a certain level. Without input measures, you will find yourself in a situation like Jasmine – recognising that satisfaction is slipping, but not being able to identify what is behind the decline. If this is the case, it is difficult to remedy the situation.

While output measures are specifically tied to your business, input measures tend to be more generic. There are a number of frameworks to choose from, and one of the most robust and easy to use was developed by Parasuraman, Zeithaml and Berry (1988) and described in *Services Marketing* (Zeithaml and Bitner, 1996). The dimensions in their framework are:

- reliability;
- responsiveness;
- assurance;
- tangibles;
- empathy.

Reliability

Remember that every service has two key components: 1) what the service delivers, and 2) how the service is delivered. Reliability measures are part of assessing the first of these components. Reliability is your ability to perform your promised service dependably and accurately.

Reliability has consistently been shown to be the single most important determinant of perceived service quality across a number of different industries. Think about a carpet cleaner who comes to your home but does not remove the marks from the carpet, the courier who delivers the package to the wrong address, or the airline that gets you to Singapore and your bags to Jakarta. These are good examples of where *reliability* has let the service down.

Measuring reliability involves asking questions about the core promise you make to your customers. For instance, a car repairer might ask customers to rate the degree to which they agree or disagree with the following statements:

- I was happy with the repairs to the car when I picked it up.
- There has been no recurrence of problems that should have been addressed.
- The mechanic did what he/she said he/she would do to the car when I dropped it off.

Responsiveness

When a customer calls a service organisation, they expect helpful and timely service. For example, if an insurance agent tells you he or she will call you within 24 hours, you expect your phone to ring within that period. If you say you will post an item today, then a local customer will expect to receive it tomorrow.

These are examples of responsiveness. Typically, responsiveness is the second most critical aspect of service to customers. To measure responsiveness the same car repair service might ask its customers whether:

- the car was repaired in a timely and efficient manner;
- the mechanical repairs were completed in the expected timeframe;
- the mechanic kept you up to date with when the car would be ready.

Assurance

Assurance is a critical component of the business mix for smaller service organisations, as it is with professional firms: lawyers, accountants, architects, and so on. How do you feel when your 'specialist' has to go and ask someone else what he or she thinks the problem is?

Assurance is a reflection of your employees' knowledge, and their ability to inspire trust and confidence. Assurance is one of those highly intangible elements that often go unnoticed in organisations. This is why it is so important to measure it.

So, the same mechanical service might ask customers to 'agree' or 'disagree' with the following types of statements:

- the mechanic seemed to know what he/she was doing.
- I left the car feeling confident that it was in good hands.
- the repairs required were explained to me.

Empathy

Empathy relates to the degree of caring and individualised attention given to customers. Acknowledging a hotel customer by name, remembering a regular customer's preferences at a bar, giving due sympathy and support to a distressed coach traveller – these are all examples of empathy.

Empathy is also being able to communicate to customers in the right way. Have you ever walked into a doctor's surgery and walked out again feeling baffled by scientific jargon? If this is the case, the doctor probably hasn't shown sufficient empathy in terms of dealing with you on a level you could understand. In this way, empathy can have a significant impact on the assurance dimension you just read about.

In the motor mechanic example, here are some empathy statements that could be used in the questionnaire:

- The mechanic seemed to understand what I was saying.
- They mechanic recognised my frustration at being without a car.
- The service was warm and friendly.

Tangibles

Tangibles are the appearance of all physical facilities, equipment, personnel and communication materials. The cleanliness of a fast food restaurant, the dress code and cars driven by pizza delivery staff and so on all send messages to the customer.

Some questions about tangibles that the motor mechanic repair service might ask its customers include:

- The workplace looked well organised and professional.
- The mechanic was clean and well presented when he/she served me.
- The documentation was clear and professional.
- The reception area indicated that this was a highly professional organisation.

As an exercise, think about the ways different businesses have manipulated these inputs to deliberately create an impression. For example:

- A customer complaints department that focuses on empathy and responsiveness gives a clear signal to customers that its staff care.

- Photo shops that offer 'one-hour processing' differentiate themselves from other providers (24-hour service through chemists) on responsiveness.
- Mechanical repair services used to focus on reliability, but soon realised that this is difficult for many customers to judge (how do you tell whether they have fixed the problem when you first pick the car up?). As a result, many now emphasise the qualifications of their people and their clean and tidy workplaces to communicate professionalism (assurance/tangibles).

Develop the questionnaire to collect the data

You are now ready to develop your own customer satisfaction questionnaire. You know what headings to use and what kinds of questions to ask. Simply follow these steps.

Step 1 – List the items you need to measure

You have already developed this list in this chapter.

Step 2 – Develop output measures

Using the examples provided, develop 'absolute', 'expectations' and 'competitor' questions for each of the items on your list. Avoid open-ended questions (where customers fill in the answers rather than ticking a box or score), as you want to get as many *measures* as possible from the questionnaire. The open-ended questions should be available only where you do not know what responses customers are likely to give you. Often, details of a complaint or suggestions for improvement need to be open ended.

Step 3 – Develop input measures

Again, using the examples provided, create questions for 'reliability', 'responsiveness', 'assurance', 'empathy' and 'tangibles'. Once you have the questions you will need a scale. While different researchers will offer different opinions about the type of scale or questioning that should be used, the key is to decide on a style of questioning and *stick with it*. A five-point scale generally works better than a three- or seven-point scale. A good pattern to use is:

- Strongly agree
- Agree
- Neither agree or disagree
- Disagree
- Strongly disagree

or

- Very satisfied
- Satisfied
- Neither satisfied nor dissatisfied
- Dissatisfied
- Very dissatisfied

This would look as follows for the 'assurance' questions in the example in this chapter:

The mechanic seemed to know what he/she was doing.

Strongly agree	☐
Agree	☐
Neither	☐
Disagree	☐
Strongly disagree	☐

I left the car feeling confident that it was in good hands.

Strongly agree	☐
Agree	☐
Neither	☐
Disagree	☐
Strongly disagree	☐

The repairs required were explained to me.

Strongly agree	☐
Agree	☐
Neither	☐
Disagree	☐
Strongly disagree	☐

Step 4 – Reduce the number of questions

For customer satisfaction surveys it is particularly important to make sure the questionnaire is short, simple and meaningful. Short surveys are easier for customers to complete. So, too, are simple ones.

At the moment you may have too many questions. Reduce this list by doing the following:

- Highlight any duplications, and weed out the superfluous questions.
- Prioritise the remaining questions, so that the data you most require are at the top of the list. Chop off the questions at the bottom.
- Ask a sample of your customers to complete the questionnaire (in its prioritised state) and see how long it takes. If it is longer than five minutes, then eliminate those questions that were answered after the five minutes passed.
- Check to make sure that your questionnaire is balanced and that it contains a representative number of questions for each key heading.

Step 5 – Re-order the questions, and lay out the questionnaire

Put the questionnaire together in a way that is easy to complete and pleasing to the eye. If you want examples, then collect some from just about any large business that is serious about service. Hotels typically have reasonable question-naires.

Step 6 – Conduct a pilot test

Once you are happy with your questionnaire, you need to conduct a pilot test. This is simply a test to see whether the questionnaire works. You need to be sure that the questions are easy to interpret, it is easy for customers to fill in, and the survey is not too long.

If you are not near an airport, choose a set of employees as well as customers to help you test the questionnaire – you will only need a few of each. Give them a questionnaire (either individually or in a small group) and watch them as they complete each question. Note whether they look confused, or if a question seems to take a long time. Use this information as part of your discussion. You should also ask them to tell you what they thought each question meant, and go through their answers so that you can be sure that you have been given what they meant to say. (By the way, the airport thing was just a very old researcher's joke – pilot test – get it?)

Step 7 – Print the questionnaire

You should make sure that you keep the same questioning order, style and format to ensure that the results are comparable over time – which is a key objective for taking these measures.

Give the questionnaire to the right people

Many businesses fall into the trap of only speaking to customers who are 'easy' to access. Hotels, for instance, often leave questionnaires in the hotel room for guests to complete. While many of these questionnaires are well designed, the reality is that only those customers who have had particularly good or bad experiences are likely to complete them. This then becomes a sampling issue and can lead the hotel to make erroneous conclusions about their current level of service performance. The sample should therefore be as representative as possible of all customers, including:

- defecting customers (those who have left you for a competitor or are unlikely to return);
- first-time customers as well as longer-term customers;
- customers who also have experience with competitors (to provide competitive information);
- 'big' customers (in terms of size, profitability or importance) as well as 'small' customers.

Often, offering a prize or incentive to complete the questionnaire can help to ensure that the sample is broader and more representative.

Analyse the results

For most businesses there is no particular need to get overly sophisticated with the statistics. There are two kinds of analyses that are important: 'frequency distribution for each question' and 'patterns over time'.

Frequency distribution for each question

Add up the number of responses to each possible choice (eg very satisfied, satisfied, neither satisfied or dissatisfied, dissatisfied, very dissatisfied; or strongly agree, agree, neither agree nor disagree, disagree or strongly disagree). Put these responses on a bar graph. You may see the pattern shown in Figure 9.4.

This is (more or less) a normal distribution. Businesses with excellent service quality have a set of data that is skewed towards the right-hand side of the scale, while those that perform poorly have the opposite pattern of responses.

The right distribution for your business depends on the effect that you are trying to create. Have a look at the information that you have put in Table 9.4 and (before you see any actual results) create a template that shows your ideal set of responses for each question in your questionnaire. As a rough guide, the way the scales relate to your service strategy is as follows:

- very satisfied = desired end of the zone;
- satisfied = desired/middle of the zone;

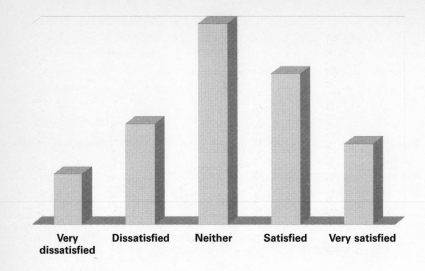

Figure 9.4 A typical pattern of responses

- neither satisfied or dissatisfied = middle of the zone;
- dissatisfied = below the zone;
- very dissatisfied = well below the zone.

For a number of your indicators you may aspire to be no higher than the middle of the zone (depending on your strategy). If the scores on your questionnaire are above your intended levels, you can celebrate, and maybe even reallocate your resources to other areas. If your scores fall below these levels then recover, find out why, and fix the causes (see Chapter 6).

The chances are that you will be prompted to act if you see the type of graph shown in Figure 9.5.

It is unlikely that you were planning to see a result like this. This pattern shows you that your service is pretty inconsistent (at best). On the one hand, you have a bunch of customers who are extremely satisfied and have loved their experience with you. On the other, you have some extremely dissatisfied customers who will probably not pay you another visit. If your frequency distribution looks like this, you will need to review the distribution of your *input* variables to try to find out where the inconsistency lies.

Patterns over time
You should add up your satisfaction data every day, week or month (depending on the nature of your business). You can then use these data to ensure that your

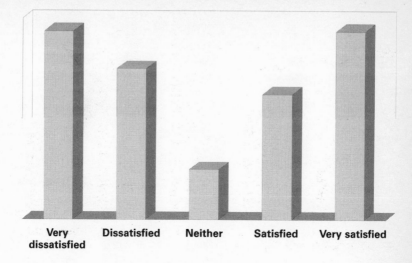

Figure 9.5   An unusual pattern of responses

business is delivering the right level of satisfaction. If not, you can recover (see Chapter 6) and fix the processes (Chapters 6 and 7). Also, you should track perceptions over time, so that you can recognise themes and trends. However, when you do this, make sure you do not fall into two common traps.

The first is overreaction. You will find that the information produced by your customer satisfaction measures changes over time, because it is highly unlikely that you will get exactly the same scores in two or more consecutive quarters. Take the satisfaction index in Figure 9.11, for instance. The shift from May to June is 2 per cent – from 30 per cent up to 32 per cent. This change is unlikely to be statistically significant (although this depends on sample size), so you can consider this shift as a normal variation in the data. You should not react to this. (On the other hand, the movement across the entire four-month period from 30 per cent to 47 per cent signals that something important has happened.)

The second trap is disguising important data. Most people use averages when they chart data over time. This can cloak real themes and trends. For example, take a look at Figures 9.4 and 9.5. These two distributions give you the same average (if you assigned a '5' to the 'very satisfied' response, a 4 to the 'satisfied' response, etc). However, the two distributions tell two quite different stories.

So, instead of using averages, a good way to measure satisfaction over time is either to track all the data, or just to plot the percentages you are most interested in. Many businesses, for instance, use the top two responses as their measure of satisfaction – so they calculate the percentage of responses to the

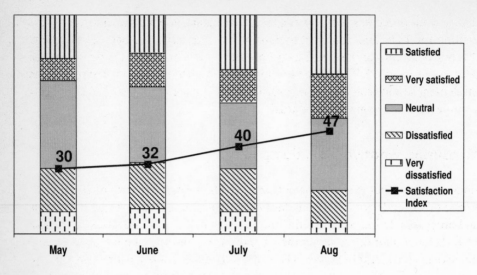

Figure 9.6 Tracking satisfaction over time

'very satisfied' and 'satisfied' parts of the scale and report this as their satisfaction measure. Both approaches are shown in a single graph in Figure 9.6.

Even those who are not particularly comfortable with numbers can perform these two forms of analysis, and generate some real insights (yes you can – go on, give it a try).

Developing and implementing service standards

Customer satisfaction measures tell you about your customers' perceptions. They are measures from the customers' point of view, and are generated externally to your business. Service standards, on the other hand, are measures that tell you how your service processes are working. They are generated within your business. Performance against service standards is an internal process performance measure.

The thinking and analysis that you have completed to develop satisfaction measures has given you two out of the three items of information you need to develop your service standards. First, you know what the customer values the most (see Table 9.3), so you can emphasise the processes that deliver those outcomes. Second, you know what level of performance is expected within your zone of tolerance (see Table 9.4).

You now need the third piece of information. You need to know whether your processes are capable of delivering that level of performance. There is no use promising customers that you can fix their dripping tap within 24 hours if, in reality, your processes perform at a level that means you are going to keep them waiting for 48 hours. You need to understand your current processes, and then, if required, improve performance to provide your chosen level of service (see later in this chapter). There are two steps that you need to follow to develop and implement service standards: 'measuring what you are doing now' and 'tracking your performance against standards'.

Measuring what you are doing now

Imagine a pizza outlet that wants a guaranteed home delivery time of 20 minutes. While this sounds good, this standard might place enormous pressure on people and processes. In busy periods this might mean that people are stressed, the risk of in-kitchen and on-road accidents increases, and the chance of making a mistake is considerably higher. The end result is that some customers are disappointed, and the pizza outlet suffers through high staff turnover and the costs of rework.

Before you can promise a level of performance, you need to collect actual performance data to understand your current service capacity. There are two kinds of data that you need: soft measures and hard measures. *Soft* measures, such as staff friendliness and cleanliness, are difficult to measure objectively, and we will consider these later in this chapter. For now, let us begin with *hard* measures – which are anything that can be measured objectively in numeric terms. The two most important hard measures are 'service times' (where time is a critical element to the customer) and 'error rates' (where reliability is critical to customers).

In the case of the pizza outlet, for instance, they need to know:

- the average pizza delivery time;
- the average number of pizzas received over 20 minutes;
- the average number of in-kitchen and on-road accidents;
- the average number of 'wrong' pizza orders delivered to customers.

Other examples are:

- Airlines measure the proportion of planes taking off on time, the proportion of 'bumped' customers (where more tickets have been sold than seats available), and the time taken to unload airline baggage.
- An insurance firm will measure the number of abandoned calls for quotes and the proportion of claims fulfilled on time.

- A dry-cleaning company might measure the proportion of occasions where garments are not ready on time and the number of customer complaints or returned items.

Take a look at items that are important to your customers (see Table 9.4), and therefore are important to measure. Now design a way to measure each of the items. The chances are that this will be a straightforward matter of counting how often activities occur for each of the items and/or how long these activities take, and then developing a way to record these data on a sheet or screen. Obviously, you won't want to measure all day every day, but you may wish to take a sample at different times over a couple of days. Once you have developed a way to gather the information you need, you are ready to track your performance.

Tracking your performance against standards

The key tool that you can use to measure service standards (of *hard* measures) is the control chart. A control chart is simply a means of mapping the average time or error rate for various processes over time to help determine normal service capabilities, and the sources of process variation. There are seven key steps to constructing a control chart.

Step 1 – Define your measures
Choose one or several aspects of the interaction that you want to measure that are both revealing and can be readily counted. These will be time (how long something takes), volumes (how many) and quality (waste, defects).

Step 2 – Collect the data
Take a sample of measures across each for a relevant time period for your business. This period might be time of day; day of week; week of year; or even month of year. Try to make sure that the sample is taken consistently every time. If you are *timing* processes, aim for a sample of between 10 and 30 measures per period. If you are *counting error rates*, be sure also to take a count of all services completed in that timeframe.

Step 3 – Analyse the data
Now calculate the *average* for time-based or volume measures for each period. To do this, simply add up all the times you have recorded and divide by how many measures you took in that period.

Calculate the *proportion* of errors by taking the number of errors and dividing them by the total number of service interactions conducted in that period. For example: A pizza outlet takes 10 measures during peak hours every day of the week. On Monday, the delivery times are 16 minutes; 13 minutes; 27 minutes; 20 minutes; 17 minutes; 12 minutes; 15 minutes; 21 minutes; 20 minutes; 24 minutes; and 14 minutes. The average for Monday is $(16 + 13 + 27 + 17 + 12 + 15 + 21 + 20 + 24 + 14)/10 = 19.9$ minutes (or 19 minutes and 54 seconds). The same outlet had two complaints from customers who received the wrong order that evening. A total of 47 pizzas were delivered that evening, so the proportion of wrong orders is $2/47 \times 100 = 4.25\%$.

Step 4 – Create the chart

Next, map these measures on a chart with the periods sampled across the bottom and the actual measures plotted against the vertical axis (see the example below). As the measures for each process are different, you will need to construct a chart to map each of the processes you are measuring.

Step 5 – Calculate the averages

Now calculate the average of all of the points you have plotted. In this example of pizza delivery times, the calculation is the average of the points plotted for Monday through to Sunday. Show this average on the graph by drawing a line across the graph at that point. This line represents your current average level of service across the relevant time periods and is your best proxy of current service performance.

Step 6 – Develop upper and lower service limits

Now you need to develop upper and lower service limits by reviewing the graph. An upper service limit will define the maximum process tolerance – in this case, pizza delivery time for the business. Consider how many points lie above that line in your small sample. You would hope that this is fewer than 5 per cent of the cases. Draw a lower service limit on the graph – this line will determine the minimum level of performance. In the case of the pizza delivery example, the business would not want to encourage reckless driving, or a service speed that jeopardised good pizza making, so the lower control limit would take these into account.

Step 7 – Develop a measurement routine

Finally, you will need to establish a programme for plotting these measurements over time. You probably won't need to continue taking measures every day or every week, but you will need to take these measures again in the future to determine whether your processes are getting any worse or better.

Now you have your control chart. It provides a map of your existing service. This map helps you understand what the average service levels currently are, as well as seeing how much variation around these average service levels exists in the processes as they stand.

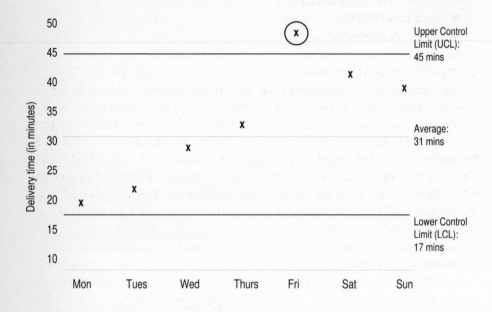

Figure 9.7 Control chart for pizza delivery times

The control chart also highlights areas of weakness or inefficiency; in this case, you can see that service standards deteriorate on a Friday.

Measures that are above/below the control limits need to be investigated to a) understand why the abnormal variance occurs, and b) make changes to bring these measures within the limits. For instance, if Friday's difficulties are a direct result of high demand for pizza on Friday evenings, the outlet might consider some of the following ways to reduce Friday delivery times, such as:

- Roster more staff on Fridays.
- Increase the price of pizzas on Fridays.

- Discount prices on days other than Fridays to spread demand.
- Discount at 'fringe' times – deals before 6.30 pm or after 9.00 pm to spread demand on Friday evenings.

There are also *soft measures* – that is, measures such as staff friendliness or the look and feel of facilities and décor. While these are more difficult aspects to measure, there are three basic ways to set standards for these service elements:

- competitive benchmarks;
- ideal benchmarks;
- historical benchmarks.

Competitive benchmarks

Using competitive benchmarks involves asking customers to compare soft service elements against those of key competitors. Once you have a measure of staff friendliness, for instance, you might then ask how your staff friendliness compares with that of other organisations similar to yours. These responses can be measured on a five-point scale (5 = much friendlier; 4 = a little friendlier; 3 = about the same; 2 = a little less friendly; 1 = a lot less friendly). You can then establish your own service standards based on your strategy (see Chapter 3) and your understanding of how important staff friendliness is in driving customer satisfaction and loyalty overall.

Ideal benchmarks

Using ideal benchmarks involves asking customers to think about the ideal service environment – and using this to establish your service standards. The process is similar to that outlined above, only now you would expect to set your standards a lot lower on the scale, because the comparative measure is your customers' 'desired' expectation levels, rather than something that is actually delivered by a current competitor.

Historical benchmarks

Historical benchmarks can also be used if your business retains customers over a reasonably long period of time. Here, the benchmark becomes 'how friendly our staff were in the past', rather than a measure against a competitor or ideal standard. Of course, you would hope to see an improvement over time, so the standards that are set might be expressed as a percentage improvement over a set period of time, or a consistent score of 'more friendly' from quarter to quarter, or year to year.

How to use measures to improve performance

Anyone who has tracked customer satisfaction or service performance knows that the scores will change over time. It is important for you to understand *why* they have moved so that you can sustain improvements, or remedy your performance (depending on the direction of the change). This part of the chapter shows you how to use all your measures to improve performance.

Terry was thrilled that the new measurement system was being taken seriously. She had worked hard to implement it and to make sure that satisfaction as well as the key elements of service quality were measured on a quarterly basis.

From the very first quarter, it had become abundantly clear that responsiveness was the key issue for the business. By focusing on setting clear standards and communicating and rewarding compliance to these standards internally, she had managed to get average delivery days down from an average of 12.3 to 8.7 days.

The impact on satisfaction and on customer loyalty was remarkable. The effect on her career was sure to follow.

Simply by mapping the pattern of input variables against the output variables, and by watching her service standards, Terry was able to identify the key areas letting Internet Music Ltd down. More importantly, she went ahead and made clear action plans based on these observations – actions that were able to turn very average satisfaction results into the highest results in the industry.

Terry's approach involved following a simple four-step plan:

- Identify areas of weakness.
- Conduct a cause and effect analysis.
- Design and implement changes to address weaknesses.
- Measure the effectiveness of these changes.

Identify areas of weakness

Identifying areas of weakness is where the input measures that were discussed earlier come into play. Take a look at the charts that Terry prepared for Internet Music Ltd (Figure 9.8). In the first quarter, she noticed that 62 per cent of customers were satisfied with the service they received. This is not necessarily a bad score, but Terry knew that it was lower than their target score, and the score achieved by their major competitor (69 per cent).

This information alone could not have helped Terry a great deal. Instead, she needed to understand what was contributing to this relative under-performance. Fortunately, she had already read this book, so she knew that it was important to measure the five service quality dimensions. These are mapped in the second chart and clearly indicated that, in quarter 1, Internet Music Ltd had a big problem in responsiveness.

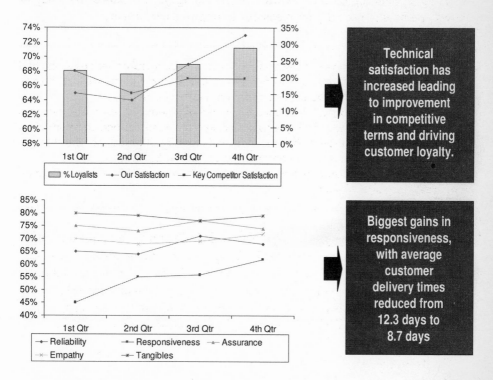

Figure 9.8 Customer satisfaction snapshot: Internet Music Ltd

Terry also knew that, on average, it took 12.3 days to deliver CDs ordered over the Internet to customers. This compared to their service standard of 10 days, which was developed using industry benchmarks. Combining all this information helped Terry to focus on where improvements needed to be made.

Conduct a cause and effect analysis

Identifying the issue is only the first step. Terry took these data and conducted a 'cause and effect analysis'. Here is a simple four-point plan to follow:

1. Gather a group of employees into a brainstorming environment. Make sure you invite employees from different parts of your business and from different levels (from senior management right down to very junior levels).
2. Make sure everyone knows the key 'rules' to brainstorming. The first 'rule' is that everyone must contribute. The second 'rule' is that all ideas, no matter how ridiculous they might seem, are recorded. The third rule is that no one is allowed to criticise any idea in any way.
3. Draw a cause and effect diagram on a whiteboard or flip chart. Define the effect you are investigating in the box on the right-hand side in clear and unambiguous language, and draw lines to capture the causes of this effect (see Figure 9.9).

SLOW DELIVERY TIME

Figure 9.9   Basic cause and effect diagram

4. Brainstorm ALL possible causes that the group believes *might* contribute to the effect you are analysing. As you do so, write these up and group them under key headings: people, processes, resources, systems, environment, materials, equipment, measures, other, and so on. Sometimes one of the possible explanations might end up having a further explanation (see the packing staff example in Figure 9.10). In this case the lines or 'ribs' of the diagram are used to explain hypothesised linkages. Use as many 'ribs' as you need to accommodate all the ideas that have been raised (you might need to redraw the diagram at the end if it becomes too messy).

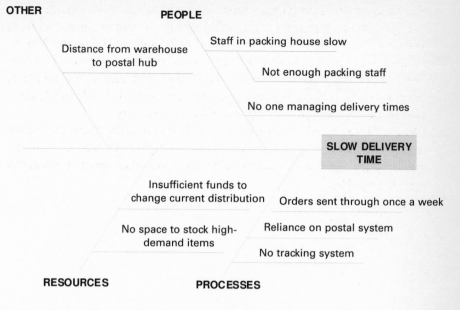

OTHER   PEOPLE

Distance from warehouse   Staff in packing house slow
to postal hub
                                    Not enough packing staff

                                    No one managing delivery times

                                                 SLOW DELIVERY
                                                     TIME

Insufficient funds to
change current distribution   Orders sent through once a week

No space to stock high-   Reliance on postal system
demand items
                                    No tracking system

RESOURCES   PROCESSES

Figure 9.10   Terry's cause and effect analysis

Here is the cause and effect analysis Terry conducted with her colleagues. Once she completed this analysis, she knew what needed to be fixed.

Design and implement changes to address weaknesses

Now that you have a number of possible causes, you need to get a feel for a) which are the major contributing factors to the effect, and b) which are the ones that you can change immediately. Evaluating each of the suggested causes in this way helps you to develop an action plan.

Here is a worksheet that Terry developed to help her determine action priorities to address the responsiveness issue (the contribution column and ease of change column are rated by management on a scale from 1 to 10, where 10 is the highest score).

The five changes Terry made immediately were:

- Introduce daily processing of orders through to warehouse, so they can be made up that evening.
- Hire an additional packer who starts at 5 pm and packs orders that evening for next morning's postage.

Table 9.6 Terry's framework for determining priorities

Cause	Contribution	Ease of change	Total (Contribution × Ease of change)	Possible actions
Slow packing staff/insufficient staff	8	8	64	Hire new packer and set responsiveness goals
No one managing delivery times	2	10	20	Nominate manager
Orders sent through weekly	10	10	100	Send orders through daily
Reliance on postal system	9	3	27	Consider other delivery options
No tracking system	1	3	3	Invest in tracking system software
Distance from warehouse to postal hub	2	1	2	Move location
Insufficient funds	2	1	2	Increase borrowings
Lack of space	3	5	15	Reorganise existing space to develop small stock area

- Create responsiveness goals for all warehouse staff.
- Take responsibility for 'responsiveness' initiatives, and establish key performance indicators (KPIs) for her own performance in this area.
- Initiate a change so that consumers get an express delivery option if they are willing to pay.

Using Terry's approach as an example, you can now develop an action list and determine priorities.

Measure the effectiveness of these changes

Once the changes were made, Terry set a target for the next quarter of customer measurement. She wanted to see the 'responsiveness' data improve from 45 to 50 per cent in the customer survey.

When the results came back, she was delighted to see that responsiveness had increased beyond this goal to 55 per cent. While the survey showed a marginal decline in satisfaction, Terry was not too worried about this, as she was confident that the process changes she had implemented would take some time before the satisfaction scores would change.

Terry was right. By quarter 4, the responsiveness measure was 60 per cent and the average delivery time was down to 8.7 days. The result on satisfaction was strong, with satisfaction up to 73 per cent – comfortably above the 69 per cent reported for their key competitor.

More important, customer loyalty had improved. The business had 6 per cent more loyal customers. The next chapter will help you realise why this, perhaps, is the most significant implication of Terry's initiatives.

10 Customers who come back again and again and again

Howard loves fish and chips. He would eat them all the time, but he saves the treat for Friday nights. Every single Friday night – after a couple of ales with the boys – Howard stops at his favourite local fish and chip shop to order his favourite dinner.

One day on the way to work Howard noticed that a new fish and chip shop had just opened in the street beside the pub. The following Friday, Howard went there to buy his fish and chips instead.

In the previous chapter we examined customer satisfaction. While it is a key measure, many businesses need to do more than just satisfy their customers. They also need to secure their customers' loyalty.

Consider Howard and his greasy dinner, for instance. Howard has chosen to try the new fish and chip shop, but not because he is *dissatisfied* with the fish and chips he has been buying or the service he has been receiving. He has simply spotted an alternative that he considers worth trying. The chances are that if he is satisfied with the new fish and chip shop, he might well continue to go there for his favourite Friday night meal.

The lesson here is that for many businesses, *satisfying* customers is not enough. Instead, satisfying customers is the 'cost of entry' to competing in many industries. Given this insight, it is easy to understand why (for some businesses) customer *loyalty* is a much stronger measure of your competitive service advantage.

Loyalty is now the 'hot issue' for leading businesses, and it is part of the 'battleground for customers' that every organisation will have to think very carefully about in the future. This chapter covers four areas:

- What is loyalty?
- How to measure loyalty.
- How to develop loyalty strategies.
- What is the value of loyalty?

What is loyalty?

Customer loyalty is easier to define by understanding what it is not, rather than what it is. In this section we will dispel some myths about loyalty, and then provide a practical model.

This is not loyalty

There are four common errors made about customer loyalty. They are as follows:

- **Customer loyalty is not just about satisfying customers**. Consider Howard's choice of fish and chip vendor. A satisfied customer may choose not to come back to your service. A loyal customer will.
- **Customer loyalty is not about forcing your customers to reuse your service.** Many organisations offer customers loyalty or reward programmes. These can range from simple initiatives such as a concession-style card (buy five coffees and get the sixth one free), or more complex offers such as airline frequent flyer programmes. The only problem with many of these programmes is that they do not drive loyalty. Sure, they might drive a short-term change in behaviour, but they will not withstand the pressure of a competitor offering a better product or service. At the end of the day, many loyalty programmes are simply handcuffs to try to keep customers coming back. The reality is that customers who are delighted with your service will come back anyway.
- **Customer loyalty is not just about behaviour.** Loyalty is more than making customers come back to your service. It is about developing a bond with customers that changes the way they think about you. Think about a truly loyal person. You might know people who are passionate about the football team they support or who drive out of their way to go to a particular pub (only to rename it their 'local'). Clearly, these individuals are driven by a deep passion, and it is this depth of emotional bond that you are aiming for when you strive for customer loyalty.
- **Customer loyalty is not driven by convenience.** Sometimes managers fall into the trap of thinking that they have a core group of loyal customers

when, in reality, the same customers continue to come back simply because the business is close to the customer's home or work. Take service stations, for instance. Do the customers really frequent their service station because of the service they receive? You will only know by seeing what happens when a more conveniently placed service station appears, or a discount petrol retailer starts trading in the area. Chances are, the customer will switch, so this type of behaviour is not about loyalty.

This is loyalty

So, you know what loyalty isn't; so let's return to the original question – what is loyalty? One way to answer this question is to borrow a framework from Richard Oliver, which is described in his book *Satisfaction: A behavioural perspective of the consumer*. Oliver has identified four key phases to customer loyalty:

- cognitive loyalty;
- affective loyalty;
- conative loyalty;
- action loyalty.

Cognitive loyalty

Cognitive loyalty is based on information provided. It assumes that the information itself is sufficiently compelling to make customers choose a brand or service. Customers might, for instance, choose to buy their pizzas from the outlet that advertises the cheapest pizza deals. This single piece of information might be the trigger that keeps that customer going back to the same pizza vendor time and time again. Is it strong loyalty? Not really, because that same customer could be attracted to another vendor if they chose to invest in advertising or price promotions.

Cognitive loyalty is therefore only the first phase of true loyalty.

Affective loyalty

Affective loyalty is a stronger phase of loyalty, and involves an emotional preference for a brand or service. This type of loyalty is built up gradually as the customer develops a cumulative satisfaction with a particular business. This is the beginning of true loyalty. You know you have it when customers make statements like 'I really like that restaurant', or 'I think they have excellent service'.

While stronger, affective loyalty alone does not guarantee that the customer will keep coming back. A more powerful bond must be created.

Conative loyalty

Conative loyalty is where the customer not only likes the brand or service, but has a strong commitment to use it again in the future. When a customer says he or she will definitely return to a service then the relationship is much stronger than simply choosing that service once, or even preferring it to others.

Conative loyalty is not quite the answer, however, as sometimes what customers intend to do doesn't actually translate into behaviour.

Action loyalty

Action loyalty is true loyalty. Here, the customer knows about the brand, likes the brand and has a commitment to reuse the brand. The customer proves this commitment through behaviour over time.

Do not make the mistake of believing that you have this kind of loyalty because you have long-term customers. One could erroneously conclude, for instance, that a customer who has been with the same financial institution for 20 years is a loyal customer because he or she has shown action loyalty. This may not be true. In fact, many customers stick with the same financial institution until they need to make a critical financial decision such as buying a house or seeking a loan. During this time the customer has certainly built up an attitude towards the business through each of the customer's service interactions. It is quite possible that the customer dislikes that financial institution, and will switch at this critical moment.

So, how do you know what kind of loyalty you have?

How to measure loyalty

In this section we cover:

- the ways to assess different types of loyalty;
- examples of different types of survey questions that reveal loyalty;
- interpreting the information.

The ways to assess different types of loyalty

You should measure all four types of loyalty. The approaches and types of questions shown in Table 10.1 are designed to address each one.

Table 10.1 Ways to assess loyalty

Type of loyalty	What it means	How to measure it
Cognitive loyalty	Loyalty generated through knowledge of the functional benefits of the service	Ask customers why they chose that service on the last occasion Find out what is important to customers when they choose to visit a service in your industry
Affective loyalty	What customers think of the service and how much they like it	Satisfaction measures Degree of likeability scales Preference rankings against other competitors Perceived quality and consistency
Conative loyalty	Degree of reported commitment to the service and/or intention to reuse	Likelihood of choosing that service again in the future Commitment scales Brand affinity scales
Action loyalty	Observed commitment to the brand	Number of times visited vs number of times visited competitors in a set time period Percentage of spending in a certain time period

Examples of survey questions that reveal loyalty

You can see in the column called 'How to measure it' that there are a number of new terms. These are simply different types of survey. Using what you have learnt (in Chapters 2 and 9) about questionnaire design, you could develop the kinds of questions that belong to these surveys using the examples of each that are provided below:

Likeability scales

Likeability scales examine how much a customer likes your business, or a specific product, or a specific service, or a location and so on. An example of the kind of question you may ask is:

Thinking about your feelings towards (insert the name of your organisation, or a specific product/service), how much would you say you like the service it provides? Would you say you. . .(circle the appropriate number):

Liked it a lot	*1*
Liked it a little	*2*
Neither liked nor disliked it	*3*
Disliked it a little	*4*
Disliked it a lot	*5*

Preference rankings

This kind of scale shows you how the different competitors are perceived. Typically, preference rankings are used in interviews and focus groups. The process is as follows:

Think about the next time you visit a (specify the type of service provider here). Of all the businesses you know that offer this type of service, which ones would you consider going to? (Make a list from what the respondent says.)

Now, thinking about these businesses, I would like you to rank them in terms of your preference for use. Give the business you would prefer most a rank of 1, the business you prefer second a rank of 2 and continue ranking them until each business you have listed has a number beside it.

Perceived quality and consistency

Questions concerning perceived quality and consistency give you information about the cumulative value of your customer's experience, both overall and over time. The questions you could ask are:

Thinking about this organisation overall, how do you rate the QUALITY of the service they provide?

Excellent quality	*1*
Very good quality	*2*
Average quality	*3*
Poor quality	*4*
Very poor quality	*5*

And thinking about the service they provide over time, would you say that service is. . .

Very consistent	*1*
Somewhat consistent	*2*

Somewhat inconsistent	3
Very inconsistent	4

Likelihood of using the service again

'Likelihood of using the service again' assesses your customers' willingness to return. A typical question is:

Thinking about this service, would you. . .

Definitely use it again in the future	1
Probably use it again in the future	2
Might or might not use it again in the future	3
Probably not use it again in the future	4
Definitely not use it again in the future	5

Commitment or brand affinity scales

Commitment or brand affinity scales assess more than a specific product/service/experience and captures information about your brand. Typical questions are:

Thinking about the (insert the name of your business) brand, which of the following best represents your feelings?

I like the brand a lot	1
I like the brand a little	2
I feel pretty neutral about the brand	3
I dislike the brand a little	4
I dislike the brand a lot	5

And thinking about your commitment to the brand, which of the following best describes your feelings?

I try to use this brand whenever possible	1
I tend to use this brand more than others	2
I don't mind whether I use this brand or not	3
I tend not to use this brand as much as others	4
I tend to avoid this brand whenever possible	5

Percentage of time or spend

These questions examine how long your customers spend with your business compared with your competitors. These questions are:

Thinking about your visits to (insert type of service here) over the past three months (insert a longer time frame if your business requires it), which of the following businesses have you used?

Competitor name 1	*Yes/No*
Competitor name 2	*Yes/No*
Competitor name 3	*Yes/No*
Our business name	*Yes/No*
Competitor name 4	*Yes/No*
Etc (until all key competitors have been included)	

(Note: when you are asking this question, you might want to put the list in alphabetical order, or if you are reading them out, switch the order around each time to avoid any bias resulting from where the brand is positioned on the list.)

Now, for each of those businesses you visited, could you tell me how many times you used that service in the past three months? (Read out list again, and write the exact number for each).

This type of question is not asking for perfect recollection. In fact, imperfect recollection doesn't really matter, as the key measure of interest is the *proportion* of visits to your business relative to the total number of visits to the category as a whole.

Interpreting the information

Using the different types of surveys for each of the types of loyalty, you can collect, analyse and track data over time. You can focus on a single item of data, and use this to drive a significant change in your business (see Figure 10.2 (page 206) and the accompanying story), and for many businesses this is a sufficient level of sophistication. However, if you want to produce richer information you may want to combine different types of data.

For example, here is a straightforward matrix (Figure 10.1) that you could produce. In this matrix the responses to loyalty questions are matched against responses to satisfaction questions. We have made up names to describe each of the quadrants and we have added data to this matrix to show what proportions of customers are truly passionate about the service provided by a particular business.

In this example there are:

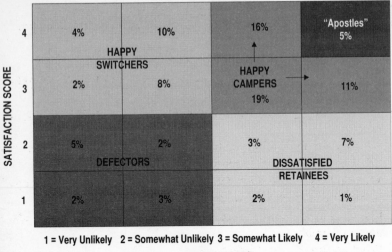

Figure 10.1   Identifying loyalty

- apostles (5%) – a small proportion of customers who are extremely happy, and so provide good word of mouth for your business;
- happy campers (46%) – a bigger group who are both happy and loyal (but not as extreme as the 'apostles');
- happy switchers (24%) – a group who are reasonably happy with the service they received, but unlikely to come back;
- dissatisfied retainees (13%) – a group who are not particularly happy, but will still come back;
- defectors (12%) – a group whom you have disappointed, who are unlikely to return and will probably spread negative stories.

This example shows that 5 per cent are a passionate group of 'apostles'. These are the customers who have 'action loyalty'. Beyond this group, there are other 'clusters' of customers. Obviously, the goal for this business is to increase the size of the apostles group by improving the service delivered to customers.

How to develop loyalty strategies

Staying with the example of the 'apostles', 'happy campers', and so on (above), once you have this kind of information in your business, there are some questions that will immediately come to mind. These include:

- What makes 'apostles' so happy?
- How is their experience different from that of the other segments in the matrix?
- What competitors are your 'happy campers' using?
- How does their level of service (technical and process) compare with yours?
- Why are 'happy switchers' not coming back – even though they are satisfied?
- Are they simply visiting you because they couldn't access your competitor?
- What about 'dissatisfied retainees'?
- Why do they persist with your service, even if they are not happy?
- Is it simply a matter of convenience for them?
- Does this mean you will lose their custom if a new competitor starts up in the same area?
- What has upset your 'defectors'?
- Was this a 'one-off' incident, or do you need to fix processes to ensure it doesn't happen again?
- Can you recover any of these customers?

These are great questions, and using the techniques in Chapter 2 – particularly focus groups – you can generate enough insights to create some powerful ways to increase the bonds with your customers, and lift your profitability. When you have this information, you can develop loyalty strategies for each of the customer segments.

Once you become comfortable with the concept of loyalty, and you are attuned to the effect that it has in your business, then you will see opportunities to deliberately change the way in which your customers view and interact with your business.

Sargeson mobile telecommunications were in trouble. They were suffering from declining profits and no one could figure out why. Maurice had been looking at the financials, but the answers were not there. The business had increased the number of customers in the past 12 months, but for some reason these customers had become less profitable.

Maurice asked to see the marketing manager immediately. The marketing manager then showed him the chart given in Figure 10.2. It was the chart that held the answer.

Maurice realised that in 2002, 47 per cent of his customers were heavy mobile phone users, and that this group accounted for 60 per cent of revenue. A year later, however, this group represented only 24 per cent of customers and only 47 per cent

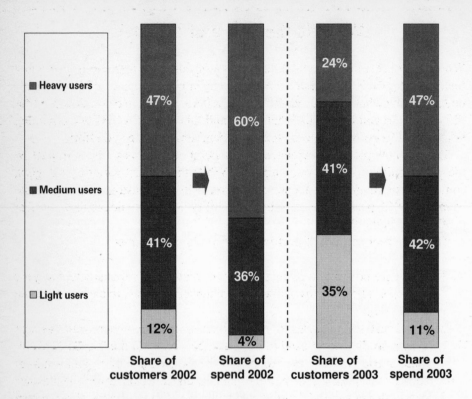

Figure 10.2 The chart that held the answer

of revenue. Somehow, the business had begun to attract lighter users who were considerably less profitable.

Armed with this insight, Maurice decided that the next 12 months would be dedicated to winning the heavy mobile phone users. However, instead of just revising the pricing 'deal', Maurice used a number of the questionnaires covered in this chapter to assess what loyalty characteristics accompanied a heavy phone user. He was surprised to find that price was not the only driver of customer choice. A big group of heavy phone users also had a keen interest in the brand and quality features. Using this information, Maurice repositioned the mobile phone offering to appeal to this kind of heavy user, and started to increase the profit per customer.

Also, when Maurice looked at the financials, he found that most of these lighter users actually *cost* the business, because the costs to service them, to send them monthly bills and to chase up non-paid invoices were considerably more than the amount of revenue they generated. He decided to segment them further into two groups: a) those that were profitable, and b) those that were unprofitable. Using the data he had collected, he developed a migration strategy to reduce the number of customers in the latter group.

What is the value of loyalty?

When you cheerfully announce that you are going to design and implement a loyalty strategy it is likely that the other people in your business will have trouble understanding what is involved, or what benefits are likely to be produced. So far in this chapter you have seen what to do, and this section is devoted to helping you to create a convincing case for the expenditure of time and effort.

There is now plenty of evidence that customer loyalty has a huge impact on the profitability of service organisations. While this impact varies by category, some analysts suggest that a 5 per cent increase in loyal customers can generate as much as 120 per cent increase in profitability. So, where does this additional profitability come from?

There are four sources of profitability from loyal customers:

1. There are no marketing costs required to attract loyal customers to your business. They already know about your service and are happy to choose it over others.
2. Loyal customers cost less to service because they know how your business works, so they don't need to ask questions, and you don't need to 'train' them to use your service properly. Take the example of a gymnasium or sports centre, for instance. For legal as well as customer service reasons, new customers must be introduced to the area and each piece of equipment before they can use the gym. This costs the business in time and effort. Loyal customers do not need this same investment.
3. Loyal customers spend more. Think about some of the service choices you make. If you truly love a particular service, you are highly likely to be willing to pay more.
4. Loyal customers tell others about your service. This is free marketing. This happens naturally.

Measuring the value of loyalty is relatively straightforward, but it does require a little maths. Let us follow through a case study to understand the net value gains you are likely to make from improving customer loyalty.

Case study: the pizza market

The pizza market is an interesting one. Imagine a household of three university students who buy pizza every Sunday night. At the moment, however, they have no reason to be loyal to any one pizza brand, so they use one brand one week, and another the following week. In fact, it really depends on who rings up to place the order as to which pizza outlet they order from.

If any pizza supplier were able to capture all the pizza business for that household, the impact on profitability would be significant. The net value of securing 100 per cent of this household's pizza occasions translates to a total of £1,040 per annum. Not only this, the cost of servicing this customer (considering the household unit as a single customer) becomes increasingly cheaper, because less time is taken to place an order when all the customer details and preferences are already recorded in the computerised database and the customer's home location is known by the pizza delivery driver.

Consequently, the profitability of this customer increases if one of the pizza outlets manages to win over the household occupants. Figure 10.3 shows this using a linear approach to calculating cumulative profitability over the year.

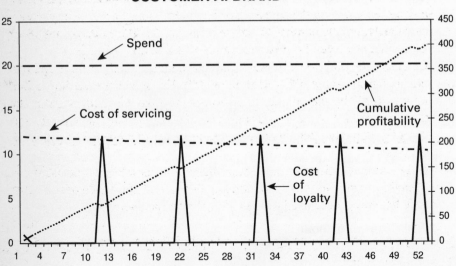

Figure 10.3 The financial effect of loyalty

Here, the net profitability of establishing loyalty (£400 per customer pa vs £102) pays off for the business. This is a simple way of looking at the profit opportunity of customer loyalty.

What would it mean to your business if you could secure 10 per cent more of the orders that are currently spread around your competitors? To calculate the potential gains from customer loyalty in your organisation, complete the following steps:

1. Find out how much the average customer spends on each visit. To keep things simple, let's assume this is £100.
2. Now find out how many times the average customer visits your business in a year. Let's assume this is 10 times. Multiply these two figures to get an indication of average annual spend per customer. In this case, the average is £1,000 per annum.
3. Next, estimate the proportion of total category expenditure this figure represents for a customer. Let's assume this is 25%. This would mean that the customer has an average of 40 interactions with the category in a year (at an average of £100 per visit).
4. Next, choose a loyalty rate. Let's assume you want to increase this rate by 10% – that is, we want every customer to use your business 35% of the time, rather than 25% of the time. Assuming your customer does not spend any more money on the category, or any more money each visit, you can calculate your new number of occasions as 35% × 40 = 14 occasions. This means the new spend of that customer is 14 × £100 = £1,400.
5. Calculate the difference between the new annual spend estimate and the old annual spend (£1,400 – £1,000 = £400). This may not seem much, but now multiply by the number of customers you have in order to estimate the increase in revenue to your business of a 10% loyalty increase. If, for instance, you have 200 customers, this amounts to a revenue increase of £80,000.
6. Now, convene a group of managers and frontline employees and ask them what they would need to do to increase loyalty, and how much of this extra £80,000 they would need to spend to achieve this increase.

You have just made a convincing case for devoting time and resources to introducing loyalty initiatives.

So, you have now come to the end of this book. You have covered a lot of ground. You have seen how to design a business that gives customers more of what they want, while protecting your capacity to be profitable. You will find that it is a journey – one without a final destination. There is always something new to know, something else to do. The secret is to use all the concepts and techniques to be responsive and flexible. The trick is never to stop improving the way in which you deliver customer service.

Appendix: Worksheets

Worksheet 1: Customer decision-making processes

Complete the following questions about your business by circling the number on the following scale:

1 = Definitely not; 2 = Probably not; 3 = Probably; 4 = Definitely; 0 = Don't know

If the statement is not applicable to your line of business, simply skip that line and move to the next. The most important part of this exercise is to be as honest as possible – particularly when you suspect the answer is 'Don't know'.

Now, going back to the table you have just completed, add up the numbers you have circled in each of the following sections and enter in the table below in the column titled 'Section totals'. Check that you have a total figure between 0 and 20 for each section.

Now calculate an average for each section. Because there were five questions to answer for each section, simply take the total you have calculated and divide that number by 5. Write the new figure in the column entitled 'Section averages'.

Now you are ready to plot your business's Consumer Decision-Making Model. This model will illustrate where the strengths and weaknesses of your business are, relative to the customer decision-making process. All you need to do is plot the section averages you have calculated on the following graph and join the four dots.

Now look at the shape of your graph, and go back to Chapter 1 to interpret what it means for your business.

Information search:

	Definitely Not	Probably Not	Probably	Definitely	Don't Know
Our business is likely to be the first one customers think of when they are asked to recall a business in our market	1	2	3	4	0
Our business is likely to be one of those customers recall when they are asked to think of a business in our market	1	2	3	4	0
More customers would be aware of our business than our main competitors'	1	2	3	4	0
Our business is easy for customers to find out about	1	2	3	4	0
We provide easily accessible information about our business that is simple for customers to understand	1	2	3	4	0

Evaluation of alternatives:

Our business is clearly different from our competitors on one of the following dimensions (more convenient; better service; cheaper price; better products)	1	2	3	4	0
The things that make our business better than our competitors are important to our target customers	1	2	3	4	0
We ensure we communicate in a way that appeals to the decision maker and key decision influencers	1	2	3	4	0
We ensure we understand the needs of our customers so we can provide them with the best service before they decide to purchase our products or service	1	2	3	4	0
Our business avoids 'over-selling' — ie we are happy to let customers walk away to competitors if they believe this is the right decision for them	1	2	3	4	0

Information search:

	Definitely Not	Probably Not	Probably	Definitely	Don't Know
Purchase decision:					
We are delighted that a customer has chosen to use our business, no matter how small or large the purchase/experience is	1	2	3	4	0
Once a customer decides to purchase products or services from us, we ensure the most efficient and friendly service	1	2	3	4	0
We make the purchase process and subsequent service as easy as possible for the customer	1	2	3	4	0
We make sure all the needs and expectations of our customers are fulfilled	1	2	3	4	0
We add value to the customer's experience beyond what they would get from a competitive business	1	2	3	4	0
Post-purchase evaluation:					
We take care to ensure all customers are happy with our service	1	2	3	4	0
We make it as easy as possible for customers to complain and always go out of our way to fix the problem even if the customer is wrong	1	2	3	4	0
We make sure repeat customers are recognised and welcomed back to our business	1	2	3	4	0
We communicate regularly with loyal customers and customers who are important to our business	1	2	3	4	0
Customers often recommend our business to their friends or colleagues	1	2	3	4	0

	Section totals	Section averages
Information search		
Evaluation of alternatives		
Purchase decision		
Post-purchase evaluation		

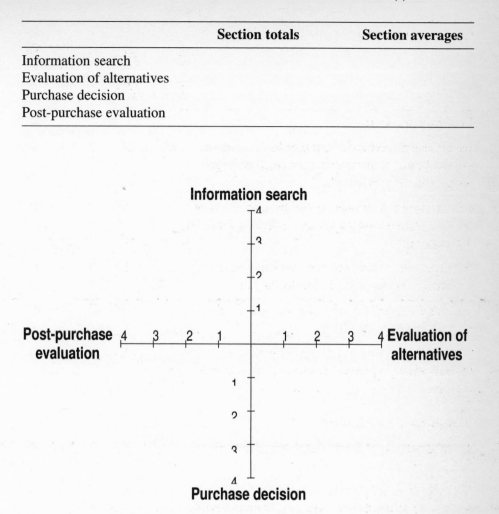

Worksheet 2: The illusion of control

This is similar to the customer control worksheet, except that here the focus is on creating the illusion of control.

Product/service	Illusions of control currently provided	Possible illusions of control that could be provided	Actions required

Now, highlight those opportunities that you could accomplish quickly, that would not cost too much and that would make a real difference to your customers. These are ones that you can introduce right away.

Worksheet 3: Customer control

Create a four-column table. Place data in the columns as follows:

- In the first column list your products and services.
- In the second column note the kinds of control that you currently provide to the customer for each of those products and services. Specify if this is behavioural, cognitive or decisional.
- In the third column note the kinds of control that you could provide (ask customers for their suggestion in focus groups and through question-naires).
- In the fourth column describe what you would need to do to introduce more control.

Now, highlight those opportunities that you could accomplish quickly, that would not cost too much and that would make a real difference to your customers. These are ones that you can introduce right away.

Product/service	Kinds of control currently provided	Possible kinds of control that could be provided	Actions required to introduce this control

Worksheet 4: Assessment of service personality

To get an accurate measure of your people you need to access the full kit of questionnaires from the supplier. However, as a quick test, create an 11-column table. Place the personality profile criteria in the first column and use the remaining 10 columns for the names of a sample of your current customer contact people. Enter their names at the top of the columns.

Then create 16 rows – one for each of the personality criteria.

Personality criteria	Person A	Person B	Person C	Person D	Person E	Person F	Person G	Person H	Person I	Person J
Persuasiveness										
Self-control										
Empathy										
Modesty										
Participation										
Sociable										
Analytical										
Flexible										
Structured										
Innovative										
Detail-oriented										
Conscientious										
Resilient										
Competitive										
Results-oriented										
Energetic										

Now, give each person a score out of five for each of the criteria. Use a scale so that 1 = fully meets the description, 3 = partially meets the description, 5 = does not meet the description. Use the scores 4 and 2 for a bit of shading. Enter your scores in the table.

Have a look at the distribution of the scores. If there are individuals who score poorly on many aspects of the profile then they may find the customer contact role difficult. If all people score poorly on the same characteristic then you probably have a common problem. If you have an unacceptable number of low scores then this points to the need to improve your selection techniques.

Imagine what it would be like if all your people met the profile. Well, now that you know what it is, you can use it as part of your selection criteria.

References

de Bono, Edward (1996) *Teach Yourself to Think*, Penguin, London

Fitzsimmons, James A and Fitzsimmons, Mona J (1994) *Service Management for Competitive Advantage*, McGraw-Hill, New York

Kotter, John and Heskitt, James (1992) *Corporate Culture and Performance*, Free Press, New York

Lake, Neville (1999) *The Third Principle: How to get 20% more out of your business*, Business & Professional Publishing, Sydney

Lake, Neville (2002) *The Strategic Planning Workbook*, Kogan Page, London

Oliver, Richard (1997) *Satisfaction: A behavioural perspective of the consumer*, McGraw-Hill, New York

Parasuraman, A, Zeithaml, V Z and Berry, L L (1988) SERVQUAL: a multiple-item scale for measuring consumer perceptions of service quality, *Journal of Retailing*, **64** (1), pp 12–40

Zeithaml, V A and Bitner, MJ (1996) *Services Marketing*, McGraw-Hill, New York

Index

absolute importance analysis 45–46
absolute measures 174
adequate service expectations 168–69
advanced research 41
affinity groups 36–37
assurance measures 176–77

barriers 94–96
behavioural control 16
benchmarks 189
   competitive 189
   historical 189
   ideal 189
brand affinity scales 202

career impact consequences 66
cash consequences 66
cause and effect analysis 191–95
   conducting 191–93
   designing and implementing changes
      to address weaknesses shown
      in 193–94
   measuring effect of changes 194–95
change 64–71, 193–95
   communication 71
   design and implementation to address
      weaknesses 193
   developing an implementation plan
      67

early wins 70
having a clear purpose 64–65
limiting objectives 66
measuring effectiveness of 194–95
preparing for 68–69
right team 70
strong purpose 67
cognitive control 17
competitive benchmarks 189
competitors 46–52, 156, 159
   competitive benchmarks 189
   current performance level 46–49
   information about 34, 51–52
   locating near 155, 159
   measures 174–75
complaints 119–28, 171
   analysing 124
   creating a 'do not walk past' attitude
      121–22
   free research 120–21, 171
   improving service processes 123–25
   information about 171
   managing 119–22
   recovery strategy 125–28
   stimulating 120–21
   using positively 119–20
conflict groups 37
consequences 66
   career impact 66

consequences *continued*
  cash 66
  credibility 66
  introducing 66
control 16–19, 150, 214
  behavioural 16
  cognitive 17
  decisional 17
  illusion of 17–19
  introducing 19
  possibilities for customers 150
  worksheets 214–15
credibility consequences 66
culture 102–18
  developing the right 102–03
  drivers of 103–10
  empowerment of the front line
    110–16
  fear and freedom 112–15
  identifying behaviours 106–08
  management attention 103–05
  management example 105–06
  measures 115
  reward systems 108–10
  right strategic intent 111
  status 110
  supportive 111–12
  training in the rules for empowerment
    116–17
customer-centred management 89
customer expectations 11, 43, 50–53,
    166–72
  adequate service expectations 168–69
  designing service strategy 43, 50–52
  desired service expectations 168
  hierarchy 11
  influences on 52–53
  measures 174
  research 171–72
  understanding 166–69
  zone of tolerance 169–71
customer expectations hierarchy 11
customer loyalty 2–3, 126, 196–209

four key phases of 198–99
  developing strategies 204–06
  generating 2–3
  good recovery, following a problem
    126
  identifying and interpreting 203–04
  measuring 199–203
  value of 207–09
  what it is 197–99
customer research 20–41
  advanced 41
  affinity groups 36–37
  conflict groups 37
  experiencing 22
  external 40–41
  focus groups 26–36
  observation 20–22
  pyramid groups™ 37–38
  qualitative 26–38
  quantitative 38–40
  talking 24–26
  see also questionnaires
customer satisfaction 16–19, 75, 115,
    165–95
  cause and effect analysis 191–93
  collecting the right information 75
  desire for control 16–19
  how to improve performance 190–95
  measures that emphasise 115
  measuring 166–75
  questionnaires 178–84
  service standards 184–89
customer service 13–14, 42–49, 56–71,
    129–53
  absolute importance analysis 45–46
  comparative level 47, 49
  competitive level 47, 48
  compliance level 48, 49
  consequence analysis 61–62
  decision process 13–14
  determining right level of 42
  market future analysis 58–59
  relative importance analysis 46

strategic priority of   44–46, 56–58
sub-optimisation analysis   57–58
successful   63–71
three ingredients for designing a
    service strategy   43–44
customer service consequence analysis
    61–62
customers   4–24, 42, 72–73, 127, 136,
    150, 169–73
    decision-making processes   12–16
    delighting   42
    desire for control   16–19, 150
    efficiency   136
    framework emphasising   72–73
    hierarchy of needs   9
    lifetime value of   127
    listening to   18–19, 22–23
    needs of   4–11
    understanding   2–19, 20–24
    wants of   11–12
    worksheet   210–13
    zone of tolerance   169–73

data   122, 124
    analysing   124
    capturing   122
decisional control   17
desired service expectations   168–69

empathy measures   177
empowerment
    fear–freedom analysis   112–15
    front line   110–17
    strategic intent   111
    structured   117
    unstructured   117
executive dashboard   74
expectation measures   174
external research   40–41

fear–freedom culture analysis matrix
    114
focus groups   26–28

advantages   27
interpreting information of   34–36
listening to   30–31
managing   31–32
probing   32–33
recruitment of   28–29
relaxing   29–30
using specific techniques for   33–34
frequency distribution analysis   181–82
front line
    empowerment   110–17
    feedback   62–63
    understanding service levels   171

'Gaps Model'   152

hard measures   185–86
historical benchmarks   189

ideal benchmarks   189
information
    collecting the right   75
    getting it to the right place at the right
        time   99
    interpreting   203–04
    processing   133–34
input measures   175

likeability scales   200–01
likelihood of using service again scale
    202
location   154–64
    access   155
    analysis   157–59
    attributes of site   156–57
    competition   155
    demography   156
    economics   155–56
    models   159–64
    nature of service   156
    site selection   154–57
loyalty   196–209
    brand affinity scales   202–03

loyalty *continued*
   identifying   203–04
   likeability scales   200–01
   likelihood of using service again
      scale   202
   perceived quality and consistency
      scale   201–02
   preference rankings scale   201
   strategies   204–06
   types   199–200
   value of   207–09
   what it is   197–99

management, six ingredients of
   97–100
managers/supervisors
   feedback from   106–10
   pathfinder   91–94
   right examples   115–16
   role   91–101
market analysis   59–61
market future analysis   58–59
Maslow's hierarchy of needs   6
measures
   absolute   174
   assurance   176–77
   competitor   174–75
   customer satisfaction   165–67,
      194–95
   developing to show performance
      172–73
   empathy   177
   expectations   174
   hard   185–86
   input   175
   leading to action   173
   loyalty   199–204
   performance improvement   190–95
   reliability   175–76
   responsiveness   176
   staying on track   71–72
   tangibles   177–78
metropolitan metric   160–64

needs of customers   4–12

observation, customer research by   2–22

pathfinder manager   91–94
patterns over time analysis   182–84
perceived quality and consistency
   scales   201–02
preference rankings scales   201
pretend managing   89–91
processes
   capabilities   53–54
   changes to   18
   decision-making   12–16
   fixing   123–26
   improving   151–53
   mapping   54
   performance   55
profit tree   72, 104
pyramid groups™   37–38

qualitative research   26–38
   focus groups   26–28
quantitative research   38–40
questionnaires
   analysing results of   181–84
   frequency distribution analysis
      181–82
   giving to right people   180–81
   patterns over time analysis   182–84
   steps in designing   178–80
queuing
   reducing perceived waiting times
      145–47
   systems   144–45

relative importance analysis   46
reliability measures   175–76
responsiveness measures   176
reward systems   108–10

service, expectations concerning
   168–69

service design
 affordance 150
 capacity management 140–43
 constraints 150
 control possibilities for customers
  150
 creating consistent mapping 149
 demand 144
 providing feedback on 149
 queuing system 144–45
 role of physical products 147–48
 'two-way' models 148
 visibility 149
service functionality
 blueprint 136–38
 customer efficiency 136
 layouts 138–40
 service efficiency 135
service processes
 elements of 130–32
 information processing 133–34
 improving 151–53
 materials processing 133
 people processing 132
service quality 151–53
service recovery
 creating stories 125–26
 effect on total profits 126–27
 power of good recovery 126
 strategy 127–28
service standards
 definition 184
 developing and implementing 184–85

measuring what you are doing now
 185–86
tracking your performance against
 186–89
service strategy
 designing 43
 implementation 63–71
 making it important 56
six ingredients of management
 97–100
staff
 criteria for selection 80–81
 knowledge/skills of 81–82
 observing 79–80
 personality characteristics 82–84
 selection of 78–79, 84–85
 status conferred by structure 110
 training of 85–89, 116–17
 worksheet 215–16
sub-optimisation analysis 56–58

talking 22–26
 customers, to 22–24
 employees, to 24–26
tangibles 177–78
two-dimensional map 34–35

understanding customers
 what you need to understand
  3–16
 why you need to 2–3

zone of tolerance 169–72

Your free 60-minute video that runs on a CD ROM

This video comes with its own software: QuickTime 6. Simply insert the disk into your CD ROM drive and it will play. If you have any problems, please contact Roy Stanton at Streamlearning on rstanton@housley.com.

The video features Neville and Kristin and covers some of the key messages in the book. The contents are as follows:

- Introduction
- Creating Your Service Strategy
- How to Run a Focus Group
- The Power of Complaints
- Understanding Rational and Emotional Needs
- Empowering Your Front Line
- Measuring Customer Satisfaction
- Conclusion, Out-takes, and Access to More Videos

You will see that your video plays on its own screen, with television-quality picture and sound. If you are not getting a perfect result, you should close any unnecessary applications that are open, to free up your computer's RAM.

You can watch the whole video through, or select the parts you want to see from the menu provided. You can also link, from the menu, to Neville's Web site or the Streamlearning Web site.

Many, many thanks go to Roy Stanton at Streamlearning (a division of Housley Communications) for working with the authors to produce this video. Check out the Streamlearning library of (currently free) videos that run online.